Word Detectives

Learning Latin Roots through Stories, Movements, and Pictures to Expand Vocabulary

Written and Illustrated by Trista Gleason
in Collaboration with LuAnn Scott, M.S. CCC-SLP

Volume 1

Word Detectives

Learning Latin Roots through
Stories, Movements, and Pictures
to Expand Vocabulary

Acknowledgements

<u>Unlocking Literacy, Effective Decoding & Spelling Instruction</u> by Marcia K. Henry

The selection and order of Latin Roots are based on Henry's recommendation in her book. For additional activities, and lists of words arranged by prefix, suffix, Latin root, and Greek combining form, please consult this extraordinary book.

Dictionary.com

This outstanding website not only provided me with numerous definitions, but it also listed word origin and history. This website was invaluable to me and is an excellent free resource for students.

Eisenhower Elementary School, Fort Leavenworth, KS

Principals Marlene Black and Cindy Wepking, the second grade team, Melissa Heinen, Cymbre Herringer, Laura Hurd, and Stacy Lee, my son's first grade teacher Susan Todd, and the rest of the fabulous faculty and staff are responsible for encouraging me to publish this series. They taught my children, and they taught me. Thank you.

LuAnn Scott and Joel P. Gleason

My mother, LuAnn, read to me. She taught me how to read and to love it when I was a little girl. My mother also shared her passion for teaching. Her love of her profession is contagious.

Following a very full day at the office, my husband, Joel, spent his nights helping me come up with silly stories, taking vocabulary tests, and editing and revising this workbook. To you both: thank you, and I love you.

Mary M. Bethune Elementary, Hollywood, Florida

Principal Mary Lou Ridge, and teachers Cheryll Best, Katherine Bennett, Marta Moise, Dawn Fein and Louise Carpenter allowed LuAnn to step out of the box and develop new methods by combining parts of many different programs with the best elements of their teaching. They provided valuable feedback concerning what works and what does not work within classrooms. Thank you.

Table of Contents

To teachers and parents iv
Sticky Phonics Stories vi

Attention Students..1
Latin Roots Pretest (Vol. 1) 3
Lesson 1..5
    form..6
    port...8
    rupt..10
    tract..12
    Use the Roots, Lesson 1 15
Lesson 2..21
    scrib, script...22
    spec, spect, spic 24
    stru, struct, stry...26
    flect, flex..28
    Use the Roots, Lesson 2 33
Lesson 3..39
    dic, dict..40
    fer..42
    mit, miss..44
    duc, duce, duct..46
    Use the Roots, Lesson 3 51
Lesson 4..57
    cred 58
    vert, vers 60
    pel, puls...62
    fac, fact, fect, fic.......................................64
    Use the Roots, Lesson 4 71
Latin Roots Post-test (Vol. 1) 79

Instructor's Guide to Using the Roots 81
    Lesson 1 Guide.. 83
    Lesson 2 Guide.. 95
    Lesson 3 Guide.. 105
    Lesson 4 Guide.. 115
Pretest/Post-test Answers........................... 124

Prefix Appendix.. 125
Number Prefix Appendix 130
Suffix Appendix.. 131

Introduction

To teachers and parents:

The goal of this program is to teach children the importance of Latin roots using three tools: stories, movements, and pictures. Some of the application material could be considered too advanced for elementary students. The application material is an opportunity for a teacher or parent to demonstrate how the roots are used in words and to train students to look for meaningful parts as they encounter new words. This program is meant to form a foundation for students to organize new vocabulary and spelling information as they continue their education.

The journey to this book began when Trista started teaching her son how to read. The English language seemed like a jumble of letters. She had a hard time explaining how the letters worked because they could represent so many sounds. When she could explain how the letters associated with the sounds, her son had a difficult time keeping the rules straight.

Trista and her mother, LuAnn Scott, a speech language pathologist with over 30 years of experience working in public schools, developed a method called *Sticky Phonics* to teach children how to decode words. *Sticky Phonics* uses three key elements to make phonics rules stick: stories, body movements, and pictures. They started with the phonics rules and fine discrimination of sound production from programs like *Lindamood Bell Phoneme Systems (LiPs)*, *Wilson Reading System,* and *Stevenson Learning Skills*. Then they integrated what they learned about how children retain information through body movements from the *Verbaltonal Method* by Peter Guberina. Trista wrote memorable stories based on the SUCCES* method described in <u>Made to Stick</u> by Chip and Dan Heath, and drew simple pictures to give children visual cues. They taught children to be "word doctors" who carefully dissect long words into syllables.

This first step, *Sticky Phonics,* gave children a process for decoding big, unfamiliar words, and ensured that they were not merely memorizing the shapes of words**, but there were still many times where their explanation failed to give comprehensive reasons for the way that words are spelled. Without further explanation, they just highlighted these words as "rule-breakers."

Next, they encountered an explanation of "rule-breakers" in <u>Unlocking Literacy</u> by Marcia K. Henry. Henry explained the importance of entomology, the history of a word, and the need to understand morphemes, the smallest unit of meaning in a word. Morphemes include prefixes, suffixes, roots, and combining forms. Over half of our English language contains Latin roots. Imagine if vocabulary and spelling were introduced in a way that enabled students to categorize words by their meaning. Imagine if they received spelling instruction that helped them explain why one letter must be used instead of another when either one could produce the required sound.

Finally, Trista illustrated and wrote this workbook. *Word Detectives* uses successful elements from *Sticky Phonics* (stories, movements, and pictures) to make Latin roots accessible to elementary students. Many programs start with prefixes and suffixes, but this program, begins with the "meatiest" part of the word. Prefixes and suffixes modify words, but the roots are the essence.

Students begin the program by taking a multiple choice pretest. Students should not review the pretest. The same questions will be on the post-test which is completed after all 4 lessons. Pretest and post-test results can be compared at the completion of the program to highlight student progress.

Each root is introduced using a simple story. This story is then associated with a body movement that reminds students of the meaning of the root. Finally, the root is associated with a picture that reminds the student of the story, the movement, and the meaning. There are 4 roots per lesson. The lessons are designed to be short and simple.

The images should be copied and displayed in an area that students frequently see. The roots, meanings, and movements should be practiced frequently.

There are worksheets for each lesson (after every 4 roots). The worksheets are intensive. There is a teacher's guide with a scripted explanation for each word. The worksheets are intended to be completed with guidance and instruction and may take a few sessions to complete. They teach students to identify familiar roots when they encounter them in words. First students study a list of words with a common root, and then teachers help students learn to infer the meaning of unfamiliar words based on the clues that the roots, prefixes, and suffixes provide.

This book is meant to be a tool. If introduced early (around third grade), Latin roots can be highlighted in spelling, reading, and vocabulary, but it is never too late. The story-movement-image combination impacts multiple learning styles and makes high level skills attainable for younger students. Let's become "word detectives." Let's start looking for clues!

*SUCCES: This acronym, representing Simple, Unexpected, Credible, Concrete, Emotional Stories, is a memory tool.

**Reading programs historically waver between phonics instruction and memorization. Sight-words and pattern recognition are important elements of fluency, but as students move beyond "learning to read" into "reading to learn", a strong phonics understanding is a requirement. Both memorization and phonics are important elements of reading, but students require phonics skills to tackle unfamiliar words. A discussion of the two approaches can be found in Unlocking Literacy, Henry, Chapter 1.

Sight-words are important, but you cannot memorize the entire English language. An ability to decode is required.

Stories for Those Unfamiliar with *Sticky Phonics*

Just like this workbook, *Sticky Phonics* uses stories to help students remember phonemes and phonics rules. The following list includes some stories that may be of assistance to you in combination with this workbook.

Vowel Stars

(me̥) (me̥t)

(hḁ(ve̥n)

(hḁp)(pe̥n)

u̥n)(de̥r)(stḁnd)

u̥(ni̥(fi̥(cḁ(tio̥n)

Vowels are like pop stars in the world of letters. They are famous because there is a vowel in every syllable. When we are dissecting words, we put a spotlight "•" under every vowel that we see.

All of the consonants gather around the vowel stars to form syllables. If a vowel is followed by a consonant in a syllable, it feels squashed and has to say its **sound** (the short vowel sound). If no consonant is chasing the vowel in its syllable, then it is free to sing out its **name** (the long vowel sound). We indicate that a consonant is chasing a vowel with a ")". Consonants who chase are always <u>behind</u> the vowel.

Consonants in front of a vowel usually turn around to give the vowel a hug and join that syllable. If there are two consonants in front of the vowel, try to think of words that start with both of those consonants. If they can start a word together, then they will both turn around. The vowels don't mind getting hugged. It doesn't change what they say. We indicate a consonant hugging the vowel behind it with a "(". Hugs are always given by a consonant <u>in front</u> of a vowel.

Even when the letter "i" is free to sing his name, he tends to say his sound, so try "i's" sound first.

Guide to Pronunciations

	Vowel Name	Vowel Sound
	Long Vowel Sound	Short Vowel Sound
A	/A/	/a/
E	/EE/	/e/
I	/Igh/	/i/
O	/O/	/o/
U	/U/ or /oo/	/u/

Bad Breath E

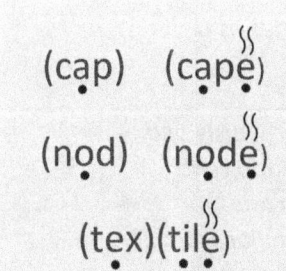

Bad Breath E loves to eat garlic. You'll find him at the end of the word. You will know he's got bad breath if he is at the back of the word and if there is another vowel in the word.

When he opens his mouth, the terrible smell makes the consonant in front of him faint and E is too embarrassed to make a sound. This means that the other vowel in the word is free to sing his name instead of being squashed and having to say his sound.

We indicate Bad Breath E with fumes "⌇⌇". Poor Bad Breath E doesn't get his own syllable. He just clings on to the end of another vowel's syllable. We write a small ")".

Poor Bad Breath E. Nobody will give him a hug. He doesn't get his own syllable like the other vowels.

But, wait! There is one brave letter who is willing to give Bad Breath E a hug. If there is an "L" with another consonant in front of him, together they will be brave and hug Bad Breath E. The other consonant must give L a gas mask so that he can tolerate the stench. How wonderful that Bad Breath E gets a hug (and therefore his own syllable) in words like "table," "bottle," and "people!"

Of course, L can't do it alone. Even though there is an "L," poor Bad Breath E still doesn't get a hug in words like "tale," "whole," and "file." He just clings on to the end of the other vowel's syllable.

Gas Masks

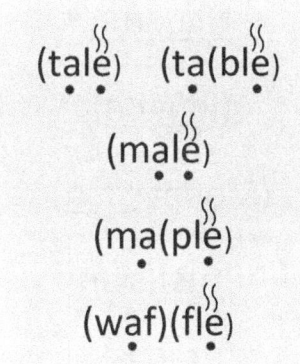

The suffix "-ed" at the end of a word transports the word back in time. Indicate a time machine by underlining it. The time machine sucks in the consonant in front of it that would want to hug the "e" in "-ed." Draw a circle around the letters and some antennas on top.

There are three different sounds that the "ed" in a time machine can make.

　　　　/t/ following an unvoiced sound such as /p/ in "popped".
　　　　/d/ following a voiced sound such as /b/ in "bobbed" or a vowel in "played".
　　　　/id/ following the letters D or T as in "seated".

Write the correct sound over the antennas.

Time Machine

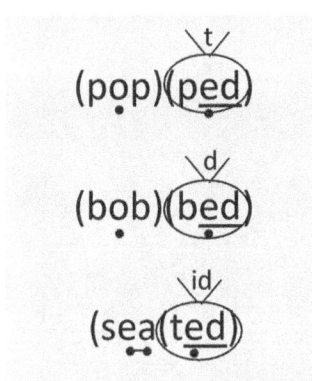

C and G are afraid of snakes. They think "e", "i", and "y" look like snakes. If C is followed by one of these letters in a word, he thinks he hears the snake say, "S-s-s-s-o, what's-s-s-s-s your name?" C is so afraid. He stutters and never quite gets his name out, "S-s-s-s-s." Words in English that begin with the /k/ sound usually start with C, but if there is a snake, then K will stand in. C is afraid in "cent" and "circle", and K takes his place in "key" and "kite."

If G is followed by "e", "i", or "y", then he thinks he hears a snake say, "S-s-s-s-o, what's-s-s-s your name?" G is so afraid that he stutters and doesn't quite get his name out, "J-j-j-j-j-j." There is not another letter to take his place, so sometimes G has to be brave. G is brave in "girl", "get", and "gift", but he stutters with fear in "gin", "gem", "gym".

Snakes

Flex Your Brain

/A/ /a/ /u/ /e/

Vowel Stars usually sing out their name when they are not followed by a consonant in their syllable, and they usually say their sound when they are squashed, but they are the stars. They can do what they want. First try pronouncing the dissected word according to those guidelines. If the word doesn't make sense, try the vowel's sound, then /u/, and finally /e/. You have to flex your brain sometimes to figure out how to say the word.

Naughty Endings

NAUGHTY

(le(gion)

(Ma(lay(sian)

(Prus)(sian)

(fa(cia

o(sten)(ta(tious)

(fi(nial)

GOOD VOWELS

(con)(sti(tuent)

(fre(quent)

o(be(dience)

(pa(tio

CRAZY 8S

of)(fi(ciate)

(gra(duate)

Toward the back of a multi-syllable word, the letters start to misbehave. They have their own set of rules. Students can memorize 7 rules and be on the lookout for 10 (numbered 0-9) endings to generate 50 Naughty Endings found in higher level words. This concept is inspired by the Ending Chart in LiPS. You should consult LiPS for further details.

Endings 0-4 are Naughty Endings. They include "-on", "-an", "-a", "-ous", and "-al."

Endings 5-7 are the Good Vowel Endings. They include "-ent," "-ence," and "-o." These endings contain vowels that behave and say what they should, but the letters they are combined with still misbehave.

Ending 8 is called the Crazy "-ates." These Naughty Endings contains "a" and Bad Breath E. The "a" can be pronounced /u/ or /A/, and the pronunciation almost always changes the meaning or use of the word. The <u>officiate</u> <u>officiates</u> at a wedding. The <u>graduate</u> <u>graduates</u> at the end of high school.

Naughty Endings are actually a combination of a suffix and the last letter of the root that it is modifying. Despite variations in spelling, they are often pronounced the same way, and understanding morphemes will help students to identify the correct spelling. Naughty Endings "-tion," "-tian," "-sion," "-sian," "-cion," and "-cian" can all be pronounced identically.

Words ending "-on" tend to be things and words ending "-an" tend to be people. This is because of the difference in the suffixes "-ion" and "-ian." The suffix "-ion" means "act of, state of, result of," while the suffix "-ian" means "one having a certain skill/art."

music + "-ian" = musician

act + "-ion" = action

The most common Naughty Endings are "-tion," "-sure," and "-ture." These last two, both ending "-ure" are the last endings students should watch out for. They are the only two endings making up ending 9.

Some Naughty Endings are two syllables. If the vowels next to each other do not work together, then draw a vertical line between the vowels to separate the syllables. Naughty Endings with an "i" that is not preceded by "t," "c," "s," "g," or "x" will be two syllables and the "i" will say /E/ like comedian, encyclopedia, victorious, menial, convenient, audience, studio, and appreciate. Naughty Endings including "tu" will have two syllables and the "tu" is pronounced /choo/ as is "punctuate" or "actual."

Future Word Detectives:

Turn to the next page to determine if you are qualified to begin training.

Attention Students:

Word Detective Vacancy

Now seeking dedicated students for intense training in word detection.

Applicants must know the secret code (how letters turn sounds into words).

- Applicants should be able to read large, unfamiliar words.
- Applicants should be able to associate sounds with specific letters in the word.
- Applicants should be able to dissect large words into syllables.

Your mission, should you choose to accept it, is to learn to search for clues in a word. **Morphemes** are parts of a word that have meaning. You have used them before if you have said, "unzip, uncap, unbuckle, stopped, seated, nodded, or bobbed." Prefixes like "un-" attach to the front of a word, and suffixes like "-ed" attach to the back. Both prefixes and suffixes change what the word means.

We are going to learn about a third kind of morpheme: root morphemes, specifically **Latin roots**. The root is the meaningful part. The rest of the word is built around it. The English language, along with Spanish, French, Italian, and others, developed from the Latin language. Latin roots are hiding in over half of our English words.

Your training will involve memorizing Latin roots and their meaning, and then detecting them inside of English words. If you know what the root means, you may be able to uncover what the word means.

Training Tools

Story: A short, simple story helps you to remember things. It is especially helpful if it is surprising, funny, or if you can relate to the characters. We will use stories to help you remember the meaning of the Latin roots.

Movement: Feeling with your body is an important part of helping you remember. The body movements will help you associate the root with a meaning and remind you of the story. Let your muscles be your memory.

Picture: Simple drawings will help you remember the story, the movement, and the meaning of the roots. You can even make a copy of the drawings and hang them up where you will see them.

Morphemes

- *Morphemes are the basic meaningful parts of words.*
- *Prefixes are usually at the beginning, roots in the middle, and suffixes at the end.*
- *Morphemes are clues to the meaning of a word.*
- *Morphemes explain spelling rule-breakers and help us to remember how to spell difficult words.*
- *12 Latin roots + 2 Greek combining forms = 100,000 words.*[*]

Word Detective training begins with the pretest on the next page.

[*] Brown, 1947

Name _____

Date _____

Latin Roots Pretest (Vol. 1)

Circle the correct meaning for each **bold** word. <u>The correct meaning is one of the options</u>, but if one doesn't stand out to you more than the other two, circle D) "I don't know". You are not expected to know what most of these words mean. How many correct meanings can you circle?

1. **transform**
A) change shape
B) robot part
C) move
D) "I don't know"

2. **export**
A) criminal
B) carry away
C) excite
D) "I don't know"

3. **corrupt**
A) broken morals
B) mechanical
C) suddenly
D) "I don't know"

4. **distract**
A) stop running
B) reject an invitation
C) draw attention away
D) "I don't know"

5. **transcribe**
A) to complain
B) signal with a radio
C) make a written copy
D) "I don't know"

6. **spectacle**
A) obeying laws
B) a public sight
C) fishing gear
D) "I don't know"

7. **structure**
A) a building
B) impressive action
C) a German pastry
D) "I don't know"

8. **inflection**
A) difficulty moving
B) curve in voice pitch
C) splattered paint
D) "I don't know"

9. **dictate**
A) tell one what to do
B) dislike a food
C) unpleasant
D) "I don't know"

10. **conifer**
A) discuss together
B) bearing pinecones
C) undesirable acquaintance
D) "I don't know"

11. **emit**
A) undo an error
B) frog anatomy
C) send forth
D) "I don't know"

12. **aqueduct**
A) flightless bird
B) blue-green coloring
C) device to lead water
D) "I don't know"

13. **credible**
A) easily made
B) worthy of belief
C) able to be eaten
D) "I don't know"

14. **divert**
A) turn from a path
B) journey underwater
C) intersect
D) "I don't know"

15. **propulsion**
A) agreement
B) pushing forward
C) pulling back
D) "I don't know"

16. **facile**
A) easily done
B) eyes, nose, or lips
C) waste products
D) "I don't know"

You don't need to go over your answers now. Save them to compare to your Post-test. See how much you learn in your Word Detective Training!

Lesson 1
form, port, rupt, tract

Lesson 1

form

"Our informant told us you would be here. Gummy Bears are not allowed in this sector. You must conform to our laws," said the man in uniform.

"I was misinformed!" I yelled.

He pulled out his transformer ray-gun and zapped me. I smelled burning sugar and looked down at what used to be my torso. It was deformed.

If only I had formulated a better plan.

"I'll come quietly if you make a formal promise to reshape my damaged form."

Can you think of any more words that contain the Latin root "form"?

Movement: Imagine you are shaping the gummy bear's melting torso. Put your hands in front of your face with your fingers curved. Imaging shaping the round belly as you move your hands up and around. Think of the root "form" as you shape the belly.

form

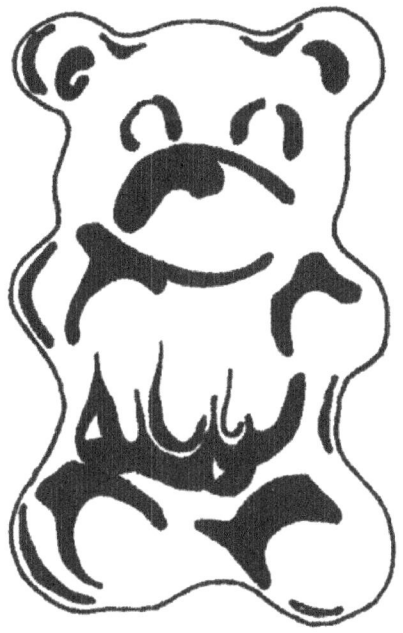

to shape

Form means "to shape."
Form [do the move] to shape.

Lesson 1

form, port, rupt, tract

port

I wish I had a portal at my house. Instead of carrying everything I could put it on the pad, and, "ZAP!" it would be transported to a new location.

I wouldn't have to worry about luggage at the airport. I could teleport it to my destination. In fact, the airport would be rather unimportant because I could transport myself.

Can you think of any more words that contain the Latin root "port"?

Movement:

Imagine you are carrying your things from one place to another. Put your hands on top of each other, palms facing up. Move them up and over. Imaging your hands moving from one portal pad to the next.

export, import, support, opportunity

port

to carry

form

to shape

Port means "to carry."
Port [do the move] to carry.

Form [do the move] to shape.

Lesson 1

form, port, rupt, tract

rupt

The school was holding the annual Spring Festival when the principal interrupted the fun to give a long boring lecture on what the children should do to avoid becoming dishonest or corrupt when they grow up. Then the talk moved on to saving money and not going bankrupt. Everyone was falling asleep.

There was an abrupt disruption when a balloon burst. It interrupted the principal in mid-sentence. The crowd erupted with laughter.

Can you think of any more words that contain the Latin root "rupt"?

Movement: Imagine a balloon bursts in front of your face. Put your fists in front of your face with your palms facing away from your face. Open your fingers and move your hands to the side.

abrupt, corrupt, bankrupt, rupture

rupt

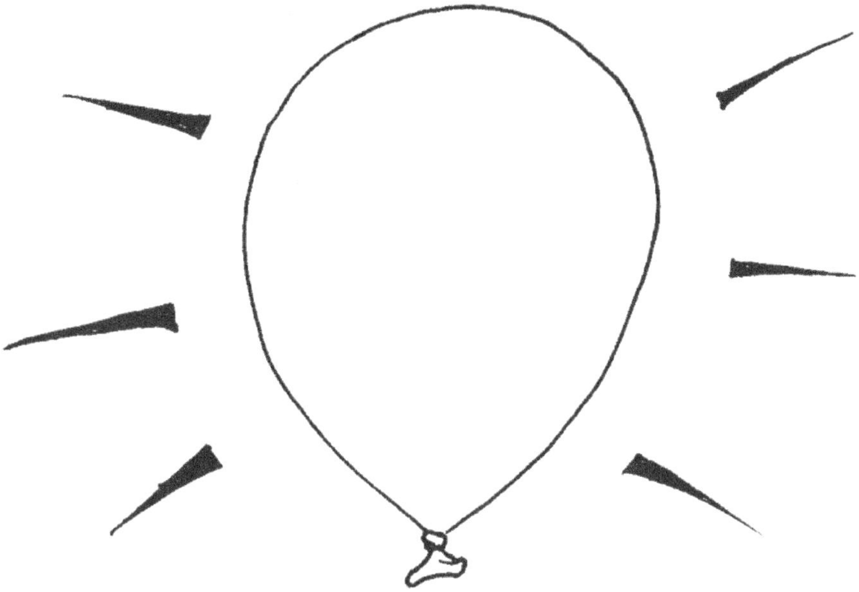

to burst

form — to shape
port — to carry

Rupt means "to break or burst."
Rupt [do the move] to burst.

Form [do the move] to shape.

Port [do the move] to carry.

Lesson 1

form, port, rupt, tract

tract

The tug-o-war competition attracted lots of attention. The students opposed a distractible farmer. He was on a tractor.

I don't want to detract from the event by telling a long, protracted story.

Can you think of any more words that contain the Latin root "tract"?

Movement: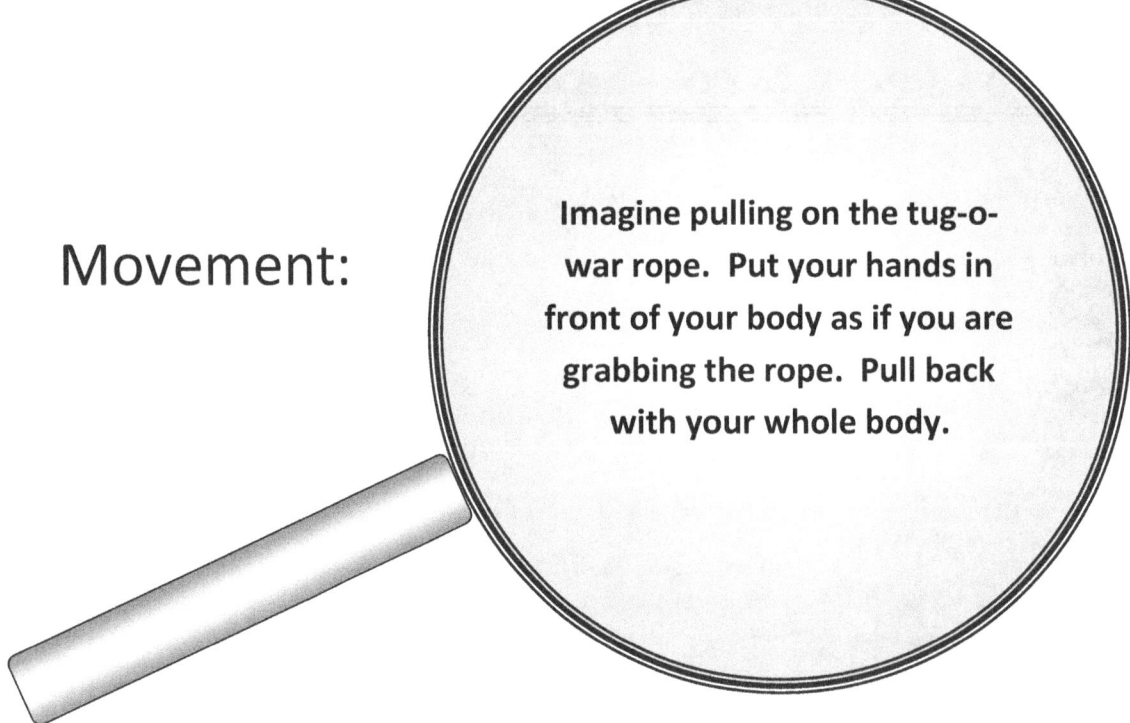

Imagine pulling on the tug-o-war rope. Put your hands in front of your body as if you are grabbing the rope. Pull back with your whole body.

abstract, contract, subtract, extract

tract

to pull

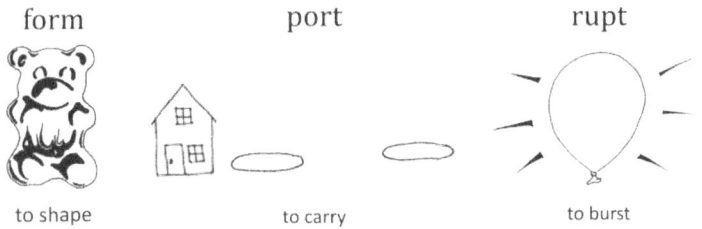

form — to shape
port — to carry
rupt — to burst

Tract means "to draw or pull."
Tract [do the move] to pull.

Form [do the move] to shape.

Port [do the move] to carry.

Rupt [do the move] to burst.

form  to shape	**port**  to carry
rupt 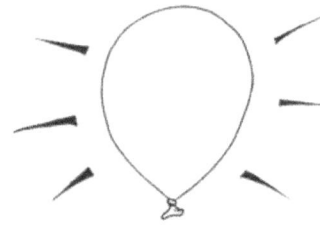 to break or burst	**tract**  to pull

Let's say the roots we have learned, and do the movements as we say what they mean.

Form [move your hands in front of your face around the round belly as you say...]: to shape.

Port [move your stacked hands up and over as you say...]: to carry.

Rupt [burst your hands apart in front of your face as you say...]: to burst.

Tract [pretend you are pulling a rope in front of you as you say...]: to pull.

Use the Roots 1
form, port, rupt, tract

Note to Parents and Teachers

- *Use the Scripted Guide on page 83.*
- *Do the worksheets <u>with</u> your students*
- *These worksheets are intended to teach students how to apply their knowledge of Latin roots, not to test them on high school level vocabulary.*
- *Use the prefixes (pg. 125) and suffixes (pg. 131) appendixes in the back of the workbook, a dictionary, or dictionary.com.*
- *Do the movement as often as you encounter the root. Repetition is an important component of memory.*

Use the Roots, Lesson 1

form to shape

Underline the Latin root in each word in the box.

| deformed | formal | conform | formulated | transformer |
| information | form | informant | uniform | misinformed |

Use clues that the prefixes or suffixes give you, or use a dictionary to match each word to a definition below. Write the word next to the definition.

_____inform_____ shape the mind or teach

_____ one who shapes your mind (teaches or provides new material) about someone else

_____ knowledge, material that shapes the mind

_____ shaped the mind in the wrong way, given bad information

_____ change shape in order to go with something

_____ one shape, identical (can be identical clothing)

_____ something that changes the shape (of itself or something else)

_____ put out of shape, disfigured

_____ shaped a method or procedure, thought of

_____ describes something that is the agreed upon shape, method, or ceremony

_____ shape

port  to carry

Underline the Latin root in each word in the box.

teleport	airport	transport
transported	unimportant	portal

Use clues that the prefixes or suffixes give you, or use a dictionary to match each word to a definition below. Write the word next to the definition.

_____ door or gate, an entrance which carries to another place

_____ carried across

_____ point from which and to which things are carried by air

_____ carry over a distance instantaneously

_____ not carrying much weight or consequence

_____ carry across

rupt to break or burst

Underline the Latin root in each word in the box.

erupted	abrupt	interrupted	disruption

Use clues that the prefixes or suffixes give you, or use a dictionary to match each word to a definition below. Write the word next to the definition.

_____ sudden change, unexpected, breaking the routine

_____ something that breaks something apart or causes disorder

_____ broke into the middle of something

_____ burst out

tract  to draw or pull

Underline the Latin root in each word in the box.

| detract | distractible | attracted | protracted | tractor |

Use clues that the prefixes or suffixes give you, or use a dictionary to match each word to a definition below. Write the word next to the definition.

_____ pulled toward

_____ able to be pulled away

_____ a vehicle used for pulling farm machinery

_____ to draw (pull) away, take away

_____ drawn out or lengthened (think of pulling the ending farther and farther forward), made longer

Do the movement for each picture. Write the root and the meaning inside the box by the picture.

Underline the root in the bold word. Use what you know about the meaning of the root to select the best definition.

1) de**tract**

A) to prefer using a treadmill
B) to record a part of music
C) to draw away or divert
D) I don't know

2) **form**ation

A) troops standing in columns or squares
B) something that makes documents
C) yes votes
D) I don't know

3) ab**rupt**

A) stomach definition
B) changing suddenly, unexpected
C) continued strength
D) I don't know

4) **port**folio

A) recommended wine pairing
B) boat part
C) a flat case for carrying papers
D) I don't know

Lesson 2
scrib, spec, stru, flect

Lesson 2

scrib, script

What does this prescription say? I know that doctors learn manuscript in school. Why does it look like she scribbled on this piece of paper? I subscribe to the theory that she is in a hurry when she prescribes my medication.

scrib, spec, stru, flect

You may see this root in either form, but they both mean the same thing.

Can you think of other words that contain the Latin root "scrib" or "script"?

The word "describe" uses "scrib" and the word "description" uses "script"

Movement:

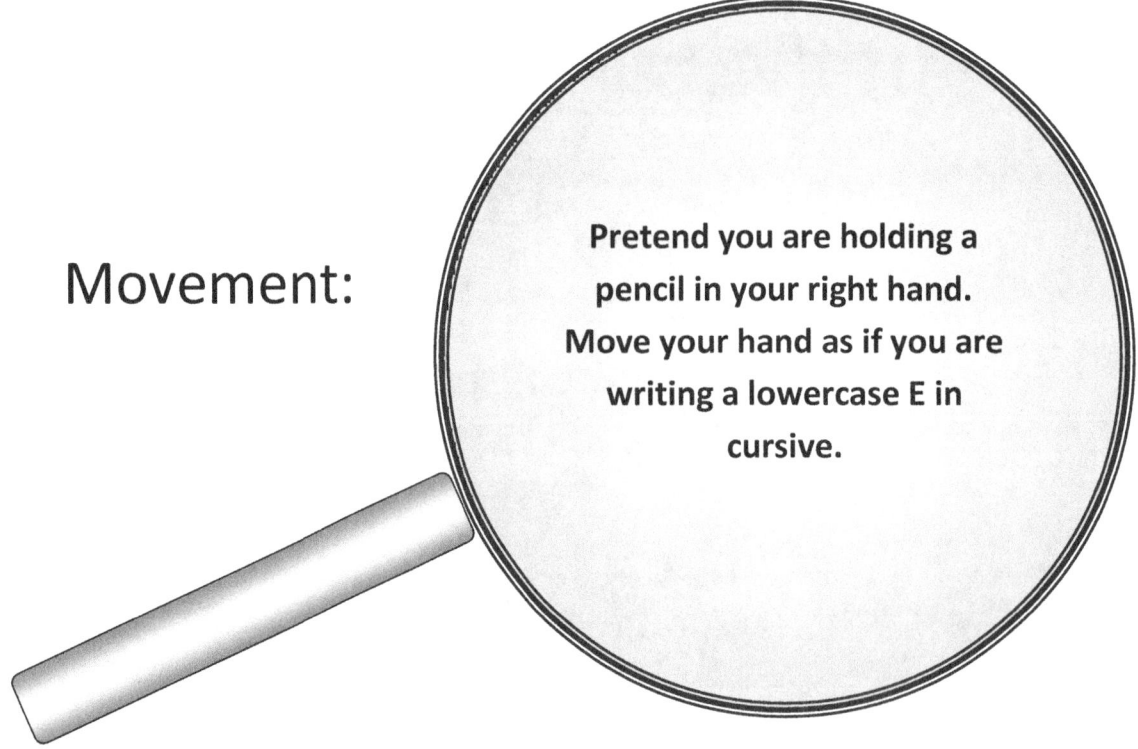

Pretend you are holding a pencil in your right hand. Move your hand as if you are writing a lowercase E in cursive.

manuscript, scripture, inscribe, describe, description

scrib, script

to write

Scrib and script mean "to write."
Scrib, script [do the move] to write.

Lesson 2

spec, spect, spic

scrib, spec, stru, flect

The men gazed over the spectators looking for conspicuous or suspicious students.

A multicolored poodle stood between them. The poodle, the school mascot, was supposed to be white.

"This suspect is especially despicable," muttered the inspector.

"Some would say that the spectrum of colors he or she used is rather spectacular. In retrospect, I wish he or she had used a less permanent dye. This species has sensitive skin. From my perspective, the perpetrator meant no disrespect," said the coach.

You may see this root in any of the three forms, and they all mean the same thing.

Can you think of other words that contain the Latin root "spec," "spect," or "spic"?

When you see these roots in words, keep in mind that the C may say /k/ as in "spectator", but if it is followed by a snake (E, I, or Y) it will say /s/ as in "specimen", and if it is partof a naughty ending, is will say /sh/ as in "suspicious".

Movement:

Imagine the inspector searching the crowd. Put your hand to your brow, palm down, and turn your head as you scan the room. After you have scanned the room, point your finger to the floor next to you as if you are telling something to sit there.

expectation, spectator, specify, specimen

spec, spect, spic

to see or sort

scrib, script

to write

Spec, spect, and spic mean "to see, watch or observe."
They can also mean "sort based on what you have seen."
Spec, spect, spic [do the move] to see or sort.

Scrib, script [do the move] to write.

Lesson 2: stru, struct, stry

After the Great Robot War, much of the country was in a state of destruction. Those buildings that remained standing had structural defects. Reconstruction efforts began.

Teams of men together with robots played an instrumental role in getting the industrial sector up and running. The past conflict did not obstruct the new partnership.

scrib, spec, stru, flect

This root has 3 forms. "Stry" is pronounced /strEE/, not /strigh/ because it is used at the end of a multi-syllable word.

Can you think of other words that contain the Latin root "stru," "struct," or "stry"?

Movement: Pound your right fist down on your left fist. Imagine a robot hammering during a construction project.

instrument, instruct, industry, construe

stru, struct, stry

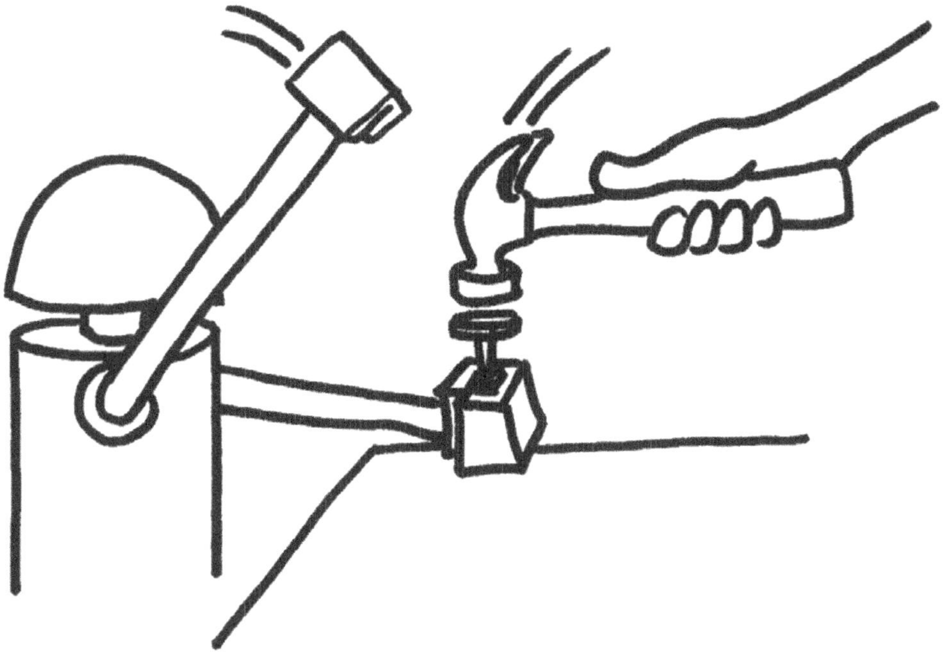

to build

scrib, script  to write

spec, spect, spic  to see or sort

Stru, struct, and stry mean "to build."
Stru, struct, stry [do the move] to build.

Scrib, script [do the move] to write.

Spec, spect, spic [do the move] to see or sort.

Lesson 2: flect, flex

The nervous mouse, kneeling on one knee in genuflection, held up a diamond ring. With an even higher inflection to his voice than usual, he squeaked, "As I reflect on what I admire about you, I am in awe of your quick reflexes and your flexibility. The world may be inflexible, refusing to think that a mouse and a snake could fall in love. I ask you to be a retroflex lady. Turn your back on what the world thinks. Will you marry me?"

The snake flexed her back, bent her head down to the brave mouse, and said, "Yessssss."

[Note: "genuflection" means "kneeling on one knee, as in prayer or a proposal;" "retroflex" means "be in a position with one's back turned"]

This root has 2 forms.

Can you think of other words that contain the Latin root "flect" or "flex"?

scrib, spec, stru, flect

deflect, reflector, inflexible

Movement: Raise your right arm over your head and curve your arm and back as you bend forward. Imagine your hand is the snake head bending down to say, "Yessssss."

flect, flex

to bend

scrib, script

to write

spec, spect, spic
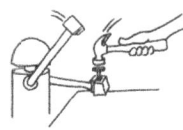
to see or sort

stru, struct, stry
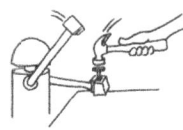
to build

Flect and flex mean "to bend or curve."
Flect, flex [do the move] to bend.

Scrib, script [do the move] to write.

Spec, spect, spic [do the move] to see or sort.

Stru, struct, stry [do the move] to build.

form

to shape

flect, flex

to bend

port

to carry

rupt

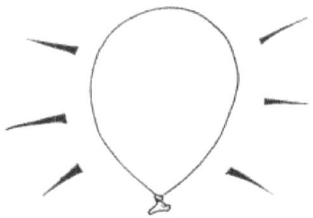

to break or burst

Let's say the roots we have learned, and do the movements as we say what they mean.

Form [move your hands in front of your face around the round belly as you say...]: to shape.

Flect, flex [raise your arm and bend your body forward in a curve as you say...]: to bend.

Port [move your stacked hands up and over as you say...]: to carry.

Rupt [burst your hands apart in front of your face as you say...]: to break or burst.

scrib, script  to write	spec, spect, spic  to see, sort
stru, struct, stry 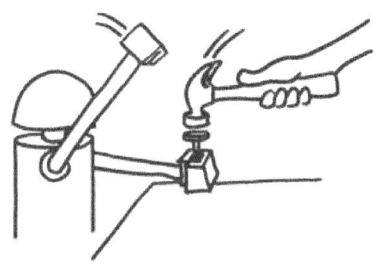 to build	tract  to pull

Scrib, script [pretend to write a cursive e as you say…]: to write.

Spec, spect, spic [put your hand to your brow and move your head as you slowly scan the room as you say…]: to see, sort.

Stru, struct, /strEE/ [hammer your right fist onto your left as you say…]: to build.

Tract [pretend you are pulling a rope in front of you as you say…]: to pull.

Use the Roots 2
scrib, spec, stru, flect

Note to Parents and Teachers

- *Use the Scripted Guide on page 95.*
- *Do the worksheets <u>with</u> your students*
- *These worksheets are intended to teach students how to apply their knowledge of Latin roots, not to test them on high school level vocabulary.*
- *Use the prefixes (pg. 125) and suffixes (pg. 131) appendixes in the back of the workbook, a dictionary, or dictionary.com.*
- *Do the movement as often as you encounter the root. Repetition is an important component of memory.*

Use the Roots, Lesson 2

scrib, script to write

Underline the Latin root in each word in the box.

| subscribe   manuscript   prescription   prescribes   scribbled |

Use clues that the prefixes or suffixes give you, or use a dictionary to match each word to a definition below. Write the word next to the definition.

_____ an order written by a doctor before being given to a pharmacist, medication order

_____ written by hand, a handwritten book or document, or handwriting

_____ was able to write carelessly or meaninglessly

_____ to write underneath, to pledge, to agree

_____ writes beforehand, gives written directions

spec, spect, spic  to see, sort

Underline the Latin root in each word in the box.

| perspective   despicable   inspector   retrospect   conspicuous   species |

Use clues that the prefixes or suffixes give you, or use a dictionary to match each word to a definition below. Write the word next to the definition.

_____ easily seen or noticed, attracting special attention

_____ able to be looked down on, despised

_____ a kind or type

_____ to look back in thought, contemplate the past

_____ causing to look at through a point of view

_____ one who looks into carefully, examines

We are going to look at words that contain one of two Latin roots. Each of these roots has multiple forms. You may find it helpful to say all of the forms, do the movement, and say the meaning after you underline the root.

stru, struct, stry 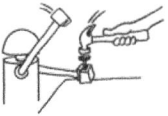 to build

flect, flex  to bend

Underline the Latin root in each word in the box.

| destruction | inflection | inflexible | instrumental | industry |
| genuflection | construction | reflect | construe | deflect |

Use clues that the prefixes or suffixes give you, or use a dictionary to match each word to a definition below. Write the word next to the definition.

_____ change in pitch or tone of the voice, bend in the voice

_____ the act of pulling down, burning, making useless

_____ to build within, activity, systematic work, productive enterprises in a particular field

_____ to be turned or cast back, as light

_____ important, necessary, like a tool to build toward a goal

_____ an act of bending the knee in reverence

_____ to bend down, turn aside, turn from a true course

_____ the act of building by putting together parts

_____ to give meaning to, to pile up together

_____ not able to be bent

Do the movement for each picture. Write the root and the meaning in the box by the picture.

The words below contain one of the eight Latin roots you have learned.

    flect, flex   form   port   rupt

    scrib, script   spec, spect, spic   stru, struct, stry   tract

Underline the root in the bold word. Use what you know about the meaning of the root to select the best definition.

1) **circumflex**

A) winding around, a vowel under a bent mark
B) a trucker adjective describing mud flaps
C) difficult academic topics, theoretical
D) I don't know

2) **uniformity**

A) different point of view, disagreement
B) obedient, following orders
C) overall same shape, homogeneity, or regularity
D) I don't know

3) **restructure**

A) to confine or keep within limits
B) to change the mode of building or parts
C) rest, take a break from activities
D) I don't know

4) **support**

A) diversion, recreation, pleasant pastime
B) to bear, hold up, carry the weight
C) a meal in the evening
D) I don't know

5) **traction**

A) an act that one consciously wills
B) parallel lines with rails
C) the act of pulling, a sticking force
D) I don't know

6) **suspicion**

A) an earnest desire for achievement
B) a doubt, a reason to look at carefully
C) stoppage of payments or debts
D) I don't know

7) **corruptible**

A) able to be destroyed, morally breakable
B) unable to be changed
C) capable of being restored
D) I don't know

8) **inscribe**

A) capacity for learning
B) not having the necessary ability
C) to write in or on
D) I don't know

9) **special**

A) different from what is ordinary, particular kind
B) a small spot or mark as on skin
C) running around a fixed point or center
D) I don't know

10) **performance**

A) a previous decision
B) a prior right or claim as to payment, choice
C) a thing that provides shape to an idea or character
D) I don't know

Lesson 3
dic, fer, mit, duc

Lesson 3

dic, dict

Peggy was the predicted winner of the Spelling Bee. She was almost forced to abdicate her title because on the day of the competition she had a cold.

Her diction was poor because of her stuffy nose, but the verdict was in, and no one could contradict the results.

Peggy was crowned Spelling Bee champ. Her teacher joked that there were indications that Peggy was addicted to the dictionary.

You may see this root in either form, but they both mean the same thing.

Sometimes the I says its name and the C is silent as in "indict" /in dIght/.

Can you think of other words that contain the Latin root "dic" or "dict"?

Movement:

Pretend you are poor Peggy trying to say the letters in the Spelling Bee. Draw a word bubble. Put your right pointer finger next to your mouth, draw a big circle in the air, and then draw a short angled line back toward your mouth.

indicate, dictator, valedictorian, benediction

dic, dict

to say

Dic and dict mean "to say or tell."
Dic, dict [do the move] to say.

Lesson 3

fer

My dad works from home and does teleconferences. Yesterday he refereed a conference between vociferous (very talkative) farmers. They discussed aquifers and fertilizer.

Embarrassed, my dad only offered a nearby book when they asked him to go and get a reference from the other room. Under the table, out of view of the video conference, he was only wearing boxer shorts.

Can you think of other words that contain the Latin root "fer"?

"Ferry" is a word with this root.

Notice the different vowel sound in "ferry".

"Fer" means to give, produce, carry, bear, or yield. All of these words have to do with "offering something." "Bear" in this case means to "grow" or "carry." A mother <u>bears</u> a child. "Yield" means "to give." A yield sign means you should <u>give</u> another driver his turn first.

Movement: Put your palms up in front of your chest. Raise them as you extend your arms as if offering the book that the dad had on his desk.

dic, fer, mit, duc

circumference, refer, infer

fer

to bear or yield

dic, dict

to say

Fer means "to bear or yield."
Fer [do the move] to bear or yield.

Dic, dict [do the move] to say.

Lesson 3

mit, miss

I paid $20 for admission to a play last weekend. Before the intermission I smelled many horrible emissions. What a stink! Maybe the man in front of me ate too many beans. He would not admit to the commission of the emission.

I would be remiss if I omitted the part where I was dismissed from the theater for throwing my popcorn at the offender. The guy with tummy trouble got to stay.

You may see this root in either form, but they both mean the same thing.

Can you think of other words that contain the Latin root "mit" or "miss"?

dic, fer, mit, duc

Movement: **Pretend you are tossing this guy out of the theater. Put your fists in front of your stomach and lift them up as you open your hands.**

transmit, submission, emissary, missionary, premise

mit, miss

to send

dic, dict
to say

fer
to bear or yield

Mit or miss means "to send or let go."
Mit, miss [do the move] to send.

Dic, dict [do the move] to say.

Fer [do the move] to bear or yield.

Lesson 3

duc, duce, duct

The Duke and the Duchess love ducks. They like to watch the mother duck lead her ducklings through their gardens and often they march in the line, too.

They educate their citizens about cautious driving to reduce duck deaths. They hired a conductor to provide music for the ducks.

Each spring they introduce the ducklings at a special ceremony and give them names. They induct the ducks into their royal pet family.

The animal "duck" is not from these Latin roots, but the animal may help you to remember the meaning of the word if you think of a mother duck leading her ducklings.
Notice that "duck" is spelled D U C K because words in English end with K or CK.
If the vowel has a buddy like UR, UN, US, OO you just use K.
If the vowel doesn't have a buddy, use CK.

You may see this root in any of these forms,
but they all mean the same thing.

Can you think of other words that
contain the Latin root "duc,"
"duce," or "duct"?

Movement:

Put your palm facing up over your right shoulder. Look behind you, and turn your head forward as you move your palm forward. Think of encouraging someone to follow you.

induct, product, producer

dic, fer, mit, duc

duc, duce, duct

to lead

dic, dict	fer	mit, miss

to say	to bear or yield	to send

Duc, duce, and duct mean "to lead."
Duc, duce, duct [do the move] to lead.

Dic, dict [do the move] to say.

Fer [do the move] to bear or yield.

Mit, miss [do the move] to send.

dic, dict  to say	**duc, duce, duct**  to lead
form  to shape	**fer**  to bear or yield

Let's say the root, and do the movements as we say what they mean.

Dic, dict [starting at your mouth draw a speech bubble with your finger as you say…]: to say.

Duc, duce, duct [motion for someone to follow you]: to lead.

Form [move your hands in front of your face around the round belly as you say…]: to shape.

Fer [lift your palms forward and up]: to bear or yield.

flect, flex  to bend	**mit, miss**  to send
port  to carry	**rupt** 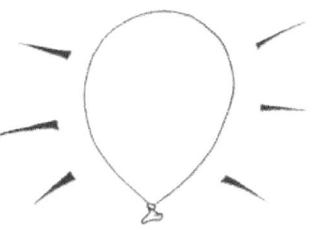 to break or burst

Flect, flex [raise your arm and bend your body forward in a curve as you say…]: to bend.

Mit, miss [toss from out from your stomach]: to send or let go.

Port [move your stacked hands up and over as you say…]: to carry.

Rupt [burst your hands apart in front of your face as you say…]: to break or burst.

scrib, script  to write	spec, spect, spic  to see, sort
stru, struct, stry 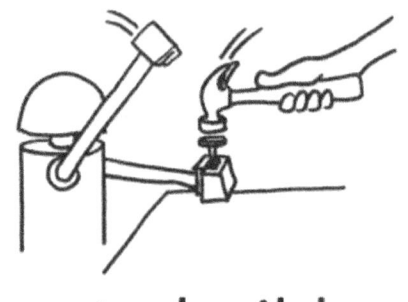 to build	tract  to pull

Scrib, script [pretend to write a cursive e as you say…]: to write.

Spec, spect, spic [put your hand to your brow and move your head as you slowly scan the room as you say…]: to see, sort.

Stru, struct, /strEE/ [hammer your right fist onto your left as you say…]: to build.

Tract [pretend you are pulling a rope in front of you as you say…]: to pull.

Use the Roots 3
dic, fer, mit, duc

Note to Parents and Teachers

- *Use the Scripted Guide on page 105.*
- *Do the worksheets <u>with</u> your students*
- *These worksheets are intended to teach students how to apply their knowledge of Latin roots, not to test them on high school level vocabulary.*
- *Use the prefixes (pg. 125) and suffixes (pg. 131) appendixes in the back of the workbook, a dictionary, or dictionary.com.*
- *Do the movement as often as you encounter the root. Repetition is an important component of memory.*

Use the Roots, Lesson 3

dic, dict  to say

Underline the Latin root in each word in the box.

| contradict | predict | verdict | abdicate | edict |

Use clues that the prefixes or suffixes give you, or use a dictionary to match each word to a definition below. Write the word next to the definition.

_____ to declare or tell in advance; prophesy; foretell

_____ to give up or renounce; proclaim away; say you don't want it

_____ to speak the contrary or opposite of

_____ a decree issued by authority; proclamation sent out to subjects

_____ declare what is true; judgment; decision

fer  to bear or yield

Underline the Latin root in each word in the box.

| circumference | fertile | referee | transfer | offer | suffer |

Use clues that the prefixes or suffixes give you, or use a dictionary to match each word to a definition below. Write the word next to the definition.

_____ one who carries others back to a source of information in order to make a decision or ruling; judge

_____ bearing, producing, or capable of bearing crops or offspring

_____ to bear under; undergo or feel pain or distress

_____ the outer boundary of a circle; the path born around a point

_____ to present for acceptance or rejection; to carry to, to bring

_____ to carry across; move from one place or person to another

We are going to look at words that contain one of two Latin roots. Each of these roots has multiple forms. You may find it helpful to say all of the forms, do the movement, and say the meaning after you underline the root.

mit, miss  to send or let go

duc, duce, duct  to lead

Underline the Latin root in each word in the box.

| permit | introduce | reduction | commit | educate |
| emissary | conduct | emit | submit | abduct |

Use clues that the prefixes or suffixes give you, or use a dictionary to match each word to a definition below. Write the word next to the definition.

_____ one who is sent out, a representative sent on a mission

_____ the state of being brought back, lowered in rank, lessened

_____ to lead in, bring in; present to another so as to make acquainted

_____ put under; let go of power and send it to another

_____ carry off or lead away, kidnap

_____ to send through, allow

_____ to send out, discharge, release

_____ to lead out of ignorance, make qualified

_____ to send to join together, pledge, promise

_____ to lead or bring together; management of others or self

54

Do the movement for each picture. Write the root and the meaning in the box by the picture.

The words below contain one of the twelve Latin roots you have learned.

form	port	rupt	tract	scrib, script	spec, spect, spic
stru, struct, stry	flect, flex	dic, dict	fer	mit, miss	duc, duce, duct

Underline the root in the bold word. Use what you know about the meaning of the root to select the best definition.

1) confer

A) a three dimensional pointed shape
B) to perplex or amaze, confuse, bewilder
C) gather together, compare, bring together
D) I don't know

2) inspector

A) one who looks into carefully, examines
B) one who teaches at a college or university
C) one who has three pairs of legs and two wings
D) I don't know

3) ductile

A) of, pertaining to, or affecting the sense of touch
B) capable of being drawn out into wires or threads
C) performing what is expected or required
D) I don't know

4) postscript

A) to put off to a later time, defer
B) additional phrase after the conclusion of a letter
C) a subterranean chamber or vault
D) I don't know

5) indicate

A) be a sign of, show, make known
B) lacking definition, vague or indistinct
C) having good understanding, comprehension
D) I don't know

6) omit

A) having complete or unlimited knowledge
B) a celestial body moving about the sun
C) fail to do, make, use, send; leave out
D) I don't know

7) infrastructure

A) built below a system or organization, framework
B) invisible light, electromagnetic radiation
C) characterized by looking into oneself
D) I don't know

8) abstract

A) utterly hopeless, humiliating, wretched
B) the posterior section of the body
C) withdrawn or separated from material objects
D) I don't know

9) deport

A) a person representing a constituency
B) to send or carry off
C) a spouse of a reigning monarch
D) I don't know

10) intermittent

A) taking place between two or more institutions
B) a time through which something lasts
C) alternately sending and not sending signals
D) I don't know

Lesson 4
cred, vert, pel, fac

Lesson 4

cred

The Incredible Extra Credit Man is a classroom superhero. He believes in hard work.

"Wherever there is doubt about the answer, I lend credence and believability. Wherever ideas need support, I find credible sources. Wherever grades are failing, I offer extra credit opportunities."

His creed may be unusual, but you have to give him credit for his enthusiasm.

Can you think of other words that contain the Latin root "cred"?

cred, vert, pel, fac

Movement: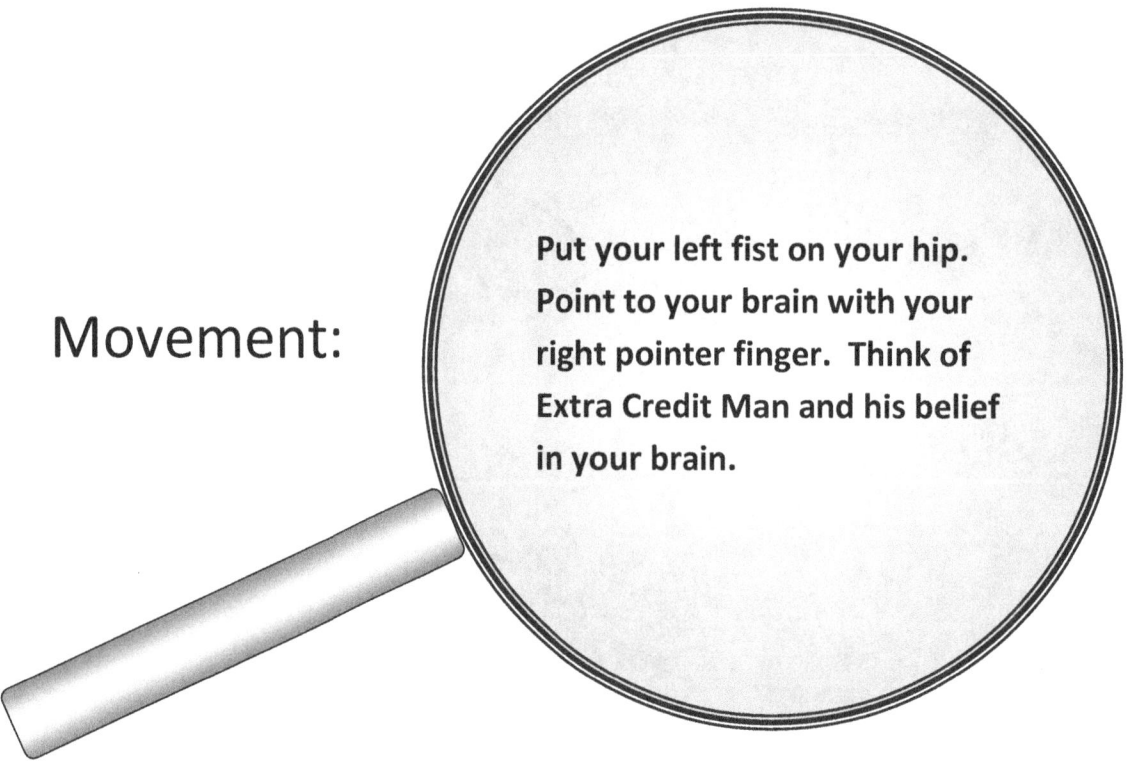

Put your left fist on your hip. Point to your brain with your right pointer finger. Think of Extra Credit Man and his belief in your brain.

accreditation, incredulous

cred

to believe

Cred means "to believe."
Cred [do the move] to believe.

Lesson 4

vert, vers

Some avert their eyes and others stare as the elephant quickly turns on the ice. How does she achieve that vertical leap or the reverse Lutz?

Originally her coach was averse to training her fearing her spins would create a vortex of wind.

She never got a bit of vertigo from her spins but other skaters would still flee for their lives. Eventually she learned to be a very versatile skater which ended the controversy.

Now, poets turn out verse after verse about the elephant figure skater.

You may see this root in either form, but they both mean the same thing.

Can you think of other words that contain the Latin root "vers" or "vert"?

cred, vert, pel, fac

Movement:

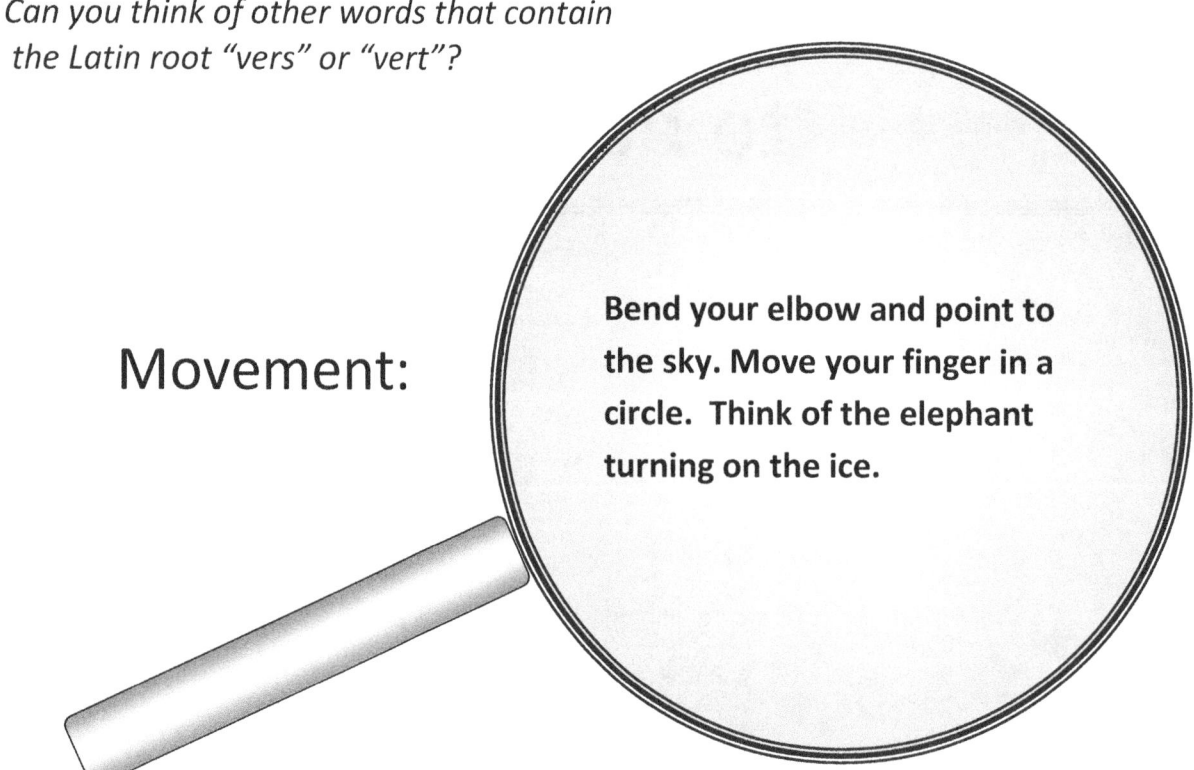

Bend your elbow and point to the sky. Move your finger in a circle. Think of the elephant turning on the ice.

divert, version, university

vert, vers

to turn

cred
to believe

Vert and vers mean "to turn."
Vert, vers [do the move] to turn.

Cred [do the move] to believe.

Lesson 4

pel, puls

Did you know you can live without a heartbeat? I am not talking about Dracula. A pulse is no longer compulsory in humans.

Heart patients can now have a pump implanted next to their heart that uses an impeller to propel blood through the body. An impeller is a part of a pump that spins inside of the pump like a propeller spins outside to move a boat forward.

The pump does not squeeze and release like a heart so there is no pulse. Do you think that is repulsive or interesting?

You may see this root in either form, but they both mean the same thing.

Can you think of other words that contain the Latin root "pel" or "puls"?

Movement:

Put your palms together in front of your heart. Push them together and force the air out from between them as if you are Dracula pretending he has a heartbeat.

pel, puls

to push

cred
to believe

vers, vert
to turn

Pel and puls mean "to drive or push."
Pel, puls [do the move] to push.

Cred [do the move] to believe.

Vert, vers [do the move] to turn.

Lesson 4: fac, fact, fect, fic

The little girl stirred her cake batter while dreaming of making the perfect sweet confection to share with her friend, the magnificent, affectionate, sparkly, unicorn. A factor she did not consider was the effect her inattention would have on her younger brother.

His dinosaur toy sailed through the air, landed in her bowl, and splattered cake batter everywhere. Her brother had manufactured a very unsatisfactory mess. Instead of baking, now she had to disinfect the kitchen.

You may see this root in any of these forms, but they all mean the same thing.

Can you think of other words that contain the Latin roots "fac," "fact," "fect" or "fic"?

cred, vert, pel, fac

Movement: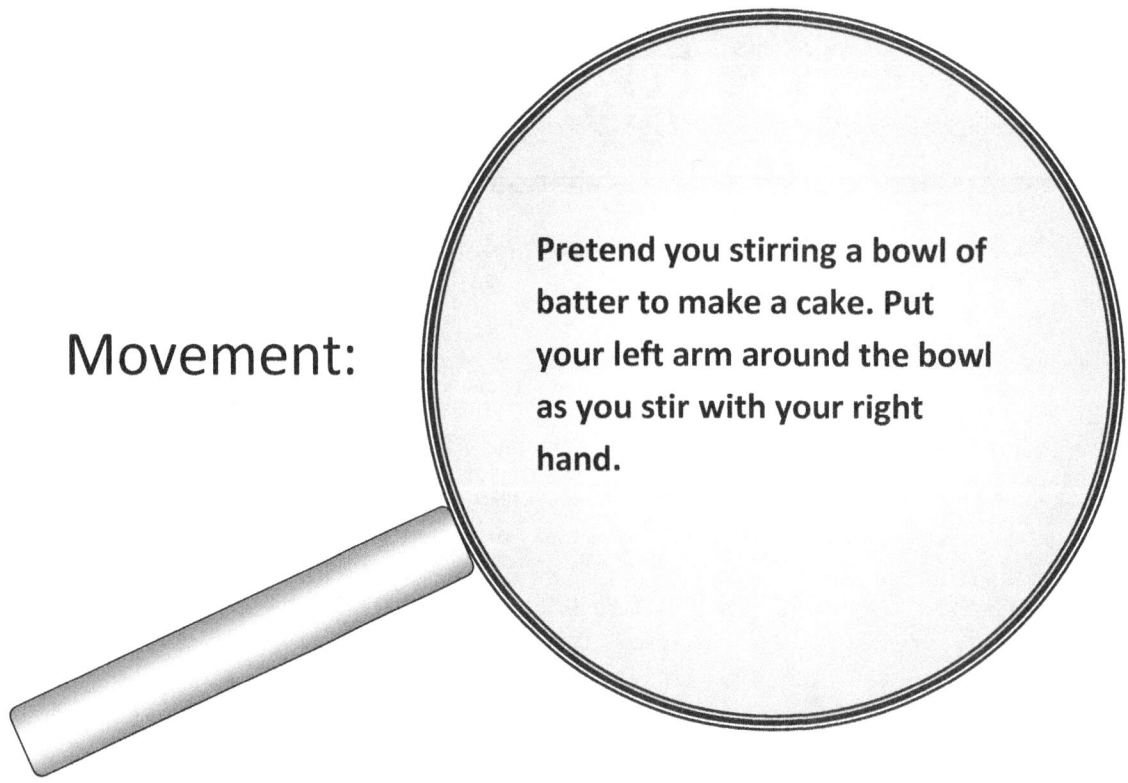

Pretend you stirring a bowl of batter to make a cake. Put your left arm around the bowl as you stir with your right hand.

fiction, office, artificial, satisfaction, deficit, facility

fac, fact, fect, fic

to make or do

cred

to believe

vers, vert

to turn

pel, puls

to push

Fac, fact, fect, and fic mean "to make or do."
Fac, fact, fect, fic [do the move] to make or do.

Cred [do the move] to believe.

Vert, vers [do the move] to turn.

Pel, puls [do the move] to push.

cred

to believe

dic, dict

to say

duc, duce, duct

to lead

form

to shape

Let's say the root, and do the movements as we say what they mean.

Cred [Point to your super brain as you say...]: to believe.

Dic, dict [starting at your mouth draw a speech bubble with your finger as you say...]: to say.

Duc, duce, duct [motion for someone to follow you]: to lead.

Form [move your hands in front of your face around the round belly as you say...]: to shape.

fac, fact, fect, fic  to make or do	fer  to bear or yield
flect, flex  to bend	mit, miss  to send

Fac, fact, fect, fic [stir the batter]: to make or do.

Fer [lift your palms forward and up]: to bear or yield.

Flect, flex [raise your arm and bend your body forward in a curve as you say…]: to bend.

Mit, miss [toss from out from your stomach]: to send or let go.

pel, puls

to drive or push

port

to carry

rupt

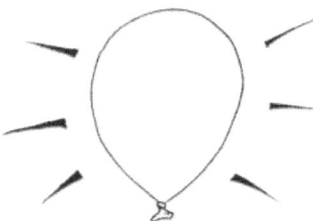

to break or burst

scrib, script

to write

Pel, puls [push your hands together over your heart]: to drive or push.

Port [move your stacked hands up and over as you say…]: to carry.

Rupt [burst your hands apart in front of your face as you say…]: to break or burst.

Scrib, script [pretend to write a cursive e as you say…]: to write.

spec, spect, spic	stru, struct, stry
 to see, sort	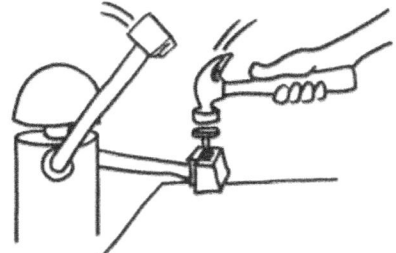 to build
tract  to pull	vert, vers  to turn

Spec, spect, spic [put your hand to your brow and move your head as you slowly scan the room and then point to the ground next to you as you say…]: to see, sort.

Stru, struct, /strEE/ [hammer your right fist onto your left as you say…]: to build.

Tract [pretend you are pulling a rope in front of you as you say…]: to pull.

Vert, vers [spin your finger in a circle]: to turn.

Use the Roots 4
cred, vert, pel, fac

Note to Parents and Teachers

- *Use the Scripted Guide on page 115.*
- *Do the worksheets <u>with</u> your students*
- *These worksheets are intended to teach students how to apply their knowledge of Latin roots, not to test them on high school level vocabulary.*
- *Use the prefixes (pg. 125) and suffixes (pg. 131) appendixes in the back of the workbook, a dictionary, or dictionary.com.*
- *Do the movement as often as you encounter the root. Repetition is an important component of memory.*

Use the Roots, Lesson 4

Name _____
Date _____

cred to believe

Underline the Latin root in each word in the box.

| credit | incredible | accreditation | incredulous | credo |

Use clues that the prefixes or suffixes give you, or use a dictionary to match each word to a definition below. Write the word next to the definition.

_____ something that brings belief to; certification; authority

_____ so extraordinary that it is believed to be impossible

_____ "I believe," a formula of beliefs

_____ not believing, skeptical

_____ trust something will be cared for, paid back; acknowledge, honor

vert, vers to turn

Underline the Latin root in each word in the box.

| converse | subvert | versatile | vertical | diverse |

Use clues that the prefixes or suffixes give you, or use a dictionary to match each word to a definition below. Write the word next to the definition.

_____ to turn a phrase with another, talk

_____ different, turned apart, a wide range

_____ turned up to the highest point overhead, straight up and down

_____ turn from underneath, overthrow, destroy

_____ capable of turning from one task to another, having many uses

We are going to look at words that contain one of two Latin roots. Each of these roots has multiple forms. You may find it helpful to say all of the forms, do the movement, and say the meaning after you underline the root.

pel, puls   to drive or push

fac, fact, fect, fic   to make or do

Underline the Latin root in each word in the box.

dispel	infect	fictional	pulse	facilitate
impulsive	compel	benefactor	repulsion	sufficient

Use clues that the prefixes or suffixes give you, or use a dictionary to match each word to a definition below. Write the word next to the definition.

_____ pushed from within, swayed by emotions, rash

_____ something that is made up, imaginary

_____ to drive in various directions, to push away, disperse

_____ the state of being pushed away, driven back, disgusted

_____ a well to-do person who makes things easier, supporter, patron

_____ throb, beat, to push blood through vessels

_____ to make or do inside of something, taint, spread impurity in

_____ having made up to the needed amount; adequate, enough

_____ to make easier, less difficult; cause to be doable

_____ to drive together (cattle), force (people)

74

Do the movement for each picture. Write the root and the meaning in the box by the picture.

The words below contain one of the sixteen Latin roots you have learned.

cred	dic, dict	duc, duce, duct	fac, fact, fect, fic	fer	flect, flex
form	mit, miss	pel, puls	port	rupt	scrib, scrip
spec, spect, spic		stru, struct, stry	tract		vert, vers

Underline the root in the bold word. Use what you know about the meaning of the root to select the best definition.

1) expulsion

A) to lay open to danger, attack or harm
B) pertaining to or characterized by an axis
C) the state of being driven out or ejected
D) I don't know

2) dictum

A) something said with authority, a pronouncement
B) disagreeable behavior
C) producer of small plastic cubes
D) I don't know

3) revert

A) return back to a former habit
B) near a natural stream of water
C) caused or derived from machinery
D) I don't know

4) traduce

A) buying, selling, or exchanging commodities
B) walk aimlessly, never reaching a goal
C) lead across as a spectacle, scorn, speak badly of
D) I don't know

5) credulous

A) a sensation of the skin as from horror or fear
B) willing to believe or trust too readily, gullible
C) mysterious in meaning, puzzling, ambiguous
D) I don't know

6) impel

A) act of a mischievous child
B) not strictly belonging, applicable, or correct
C) to drive forward, press on
D) I don't know

7) faction

A) the act of sensing with the eyes
B) a making or doing, a group, a political party, class
C) a positively charged atom or group of atoms
D) I don't know

8) portage

A) carrying boats and goods over land to water
B) a thick food made of meal boiled in milk or water
C) an overwhelming quantity or explosion
D) I don't know

9) inference

A) to make furious, enrage
B) something that comes in opposition, gets in the way
C) a conclusion that has been yielded based on reason
D) I don't know

10) scribacious

A) having a tendency to write too much
B) remarkable, outstanding, bold, brazen
C) like discovering hidden knowledge of the future
D) I don't know

Congratulations!

Take the Post-test on the next page and compare it to your Pretest.

Please continue your training with:

Word Detective Vol. 2

Word Detective Vol. 3

	Pretest	Post-test
Roots found	_____	_____
Definitions	_____	_____

Name _____

Date _____

Latin Roots Post-test (Vol. 1)

Circle the correct meaning for each **bold** word. <u>The correct meaning is one of the options</u>, but if one doesn't stand out to you more than the other two, circle D) "I don't know". How many correct meanings can you circle now?

1. **transform**
A) change shape
B) robot part
C) move
D) "I don't know"

2. **export**
A) criminal
B) carry away
C) excite
D) "I don't know"

3. **corrupt**
A) broken morals
B) mechanical
C) suddenly
D) "I don't know"

4. **distract**
A) stop running
B) reject an invitation
C) draw attention away
D) "I don't know"

5. **transcribe**
A) to complain
B) signal with a radio
C) make a written copy
D) "I don't know"

6. **spectacle**
A) obeying laws
B) a public sight
C) fishing gear
D) "I don't know"

7. **structure**
A) a building
B) impressive action
C) a German pastry
D) "I don't know"

8. **inflection**
A) difficulty moving
B) curve in voice pitch
C) splattered paint
D) "I don't know"

9. **dictate**
A) tell one what to do
B) dislike a food
C) unpleasant
D) "I don't know"

10. **conifer**
A) discuss together
B) bearing pinecones
C) undesirable acquaintance
D) "I don't know"

11. **emit**
A) undo an error
B) frog anatomy
C) send forth
D) "I don't know"

12. **aqueduct**
A) flightless bird
B) blue-green coloring
C) device to lead water
D) "I don't know"

13. **credible**
A) easily made
B) worthy of belief
C) able to be eaten
D) "I don't know"

14. **divert**
A) turn from a path
B) journey underwater
C) intersect
D) "I don't know"

15. **propulsion**
A) agreement
B) pushing forward
C) pulling back
D) "I don't know"

16. **facile**
A) easily done
B) eyes, nose, or lips
C) waste products
D) "I don't know"

Instructor's Guide to Using the Roots

This guide can be used as an instructor's script in front of the classroom or as a tool for preparation.

We highly recommend pairing this instruction with the worksheets to guide your students through the learning process. Most students will learn to identify Latin roots in words by doing the worksheets <u>with</u> an instructor. It is rare that we have found an independent learner who does not need guidance to complete the worksheets.

We recommend doing the movement each time you encounter a root. Students require repetition to store new ideas. Some may learn the meaning and how to apply the meaning after only a few repetitions, but others may require ten to one hundred repetitions. The worksheets are an opportunity to repeat the root concept while maintaining interest by examining different words.

A "☆" will remind you to do the movement as you go through the guide.

Students enjoy highlighting prefixes with one color and suffixes with another. This may be a way to enhance their learning experience. You may consider erasable colored pencils so that they can correct mistakes.

Lesson 1 Guide
form

We are going to investigate the way that roots are used in words. I am going to teach you to find roots, prefixes, and suffixes. These morphemes will all give us clues to the meaning of a word. Morphemes are the meaningful parts of a word. We learned a movement for each root that helps us remember what it means. We have not studied any prefixes or suffixes yet. Some prefixes and suffixes may be familiar to you. Thinking of words you already know may help you to figure out what the prefixes and suffixes mean. We can also use the prefix and suffix appendixes in this workbook or a dictionary to help us understand these clues.

The words on this page will all use the same root. That means the definitions will all be similar. It may be difficult to determine which one is the best fit. The root will give us a clue to what the subject of the word is, and the prefixes and suffixes will help us to choose between the similar definitions. Looking at all of these words together will help you to understand the root.

Let's say the root, do the movement, and say the meaning. Form [movement] to shape.

> First, let's go through the words in the box, underlining the Latin root "form." Notice that the root can be in the middle of a word, but it can also be at the beginning or at the end.
>
> Next we will use the clues in the word to choose the best definition from the list below. The first blank is filled in for you.
>
> The word "inform" came from Latin meaning "to shape the mind." Inform means "to teach." Think of your mind as clay. As a teacher informs you about the world, you could think of her using her hands to shape the clay into something new.
>
> This word uses the prefix "in-" which means "in, on, toward," or it can mean "not." In this case it means "toward." To inform is "to shape toward knowledge."
>
> There are three variations of the word "inform" indented below it. These will help us to see the importance of prefixes and suffixes.

Let's read all of the possible definitions, then we will be able to use the clues in the words to make the best choice.

_____*inform*_____ shape the mind or teach

      _____ one who shapes your mind (teaches or provides new material) about someone else

      _____ knowledge, material that shapes the mind

      _____ shaped the mind in the wrong way, given bad information

_____ change shape in order to go with something

_____ one shape, identical (can be identical clothing)

_____ something that changes the shape (of itself or something else)

83

_____ put out of shape, disfigured

_____ shaped a method or procedure, thought of

_____ describes something that is the agreed upon shape, method, or ceremony

_____ shape

[Deformed.] Look at the first word in the box. "De-" is the prefix, and "-ed" is the suffix. Thinking of other words with "de-" might help you to figure out what it means.

> You can deflate a ball. You might devein a shrimp before cooking it. Damage might devalue an object, making it worth less.

> "De-" means "down or away."

I know that "-ed" is a time machine [pg. vii] at the end of a word with another vowel in it, so the definition should be past tense.

☆

This word should mean something about a shape being down or away, and its definition should be past tense. Which is the best fit?

> Write **deformed** next to "put out of shape, disfigured".

Something that was not shaped correctly is deformed.

[Formal.] Look at the next word. The suffix is "-al." I know this is a Naughty Ending [see page viii], so it says /ul/.

> It means "relating to" and turns words into adjectives. Adjectives are words that describe things.

☆

> This word should mean "relating to or describing a shape." Which definition is the best choice?

> Write **formal** next to "describes something that is the agreed upon shape, method, or ceremony".

We think of formal things as being uptight with no room for doing things your own way. You may go to a formal dance where you must wear a tuxedo or ball gown.

[Conform.] Look at the next word. "Con-" is the prefix. It is usually pronounced /cun/, but it is spelled C-O-N. It means "together, with," or "jointly."

☆

This word should have something to do with "shape" and "with or together." Which is the best choice?

> Write **conform** next to "change shape in order to go with something".

Someone who conforms does what everyone else does. Someone who conforms wouldn't wear pink if everyone else always wears black.

[Formulated.] Look at the next word. I see a time machine at the end, so I know this definition should be past tense.

> Is that the only clue you need, or should we look at the other suffixes?

I see "-ulated" at the end of the word. This is a combination of three suffixes. Let's take the root and add the suffixes one at a time.

> The suffix "-ule" makes the word into a noun. When we add it to "form," we get "formule" (but we write it as formula). The meaning "shape" in this case may be better phrased as "rules or steps". A formula is a procedure that has been shaped or organized.

> The suffix "-ate" means "to cause or make." When we add this suffix we drop the Bad Breath E in "-ule", and get "formulate." To formulate is "to make a formula."

> Finally we drop the Bad Breath E in "-ate" to add the time machine "-ed" and we should have a word that means "made a formula, or made a procedure."

>> Write **formulated** next to "shaped a method or procedure".

After listening to all of the facts, she formulated an opinion. It means you organized your thoughts into a plan or a point of view.

[Transformer.] Look at the next word. "Trans-" is the prefix and "-er" is the suffix. "Trans-" means "across or beyond." If you add "-er" to the end of a word, either you are using the word to compare (as in "bigger") or you are using the word to describe a person who does something. A painter paints. A singer sings.

This word should mean "something that shapes beyond or across." Do you see the best choice?

>> Write **transformer** next to "something that changes the shape (of itself or something else)".

A transformer transforms. It makes a shape go beyond what it was originally. It changes the shape. The robot toys are called *Transformers* because they change shape from cars, trucks, or planes, to robot shapes similar to a human body.

[Information.] Can you see that this is a variation of inform? I see a Naughty Ending [pg. viii]. The Naughty Ending "-tion" tends to be part of words that are things.

This word actually has two suffixes, "-ate" and "-ion." When we combine them, we drop the Bad Breath E [pg. vi]. It is probably easier to just remember "-tion" indicates a thing rather than a person.

Which definition indented under inform is the best choice? Which one is a thing?

>> Write **information** next to "knowledge, material that shapes the mind".

[Form.] This is the root all by itself. Not all roots can be words on their own, but this one can. Form means [do the move] "to shape."

>> Write **form** next to "shape".

Form can be used as a verb. "I formed a ball out of the dough." It can also be used as a noun. "You have excellent form when you dance ballet."

[Informant.] Do you see that this is a variation of the word "inform"? The suffix "-ant" changes an action root into a noun or makes the word into a noun associated with the root. An accountant keeps track of bank accounts. A contestant is participating in a contest. An irritant is something that causes irritation.

An informant would be someone who informs. Which is the best choice?

Write **informant** next to "one who shapes your mind (teaches or provides new material) about someone   else."

Usually the word informant is used to describe someone giving the police information about criminal activity.

[Uniform.] "Uni-" is the prefix. It means "one." Think of unicorns with one horn, and unicycles with one wheel. This word should mean "one shape." Which is the best choice?

Write **uniform** next to "one shape, identical (can be identical clothing)".

We can describe things as uniform if they are all the same. If you wear a uniform for your job, then that clothing is the same as the clothing your coworkers wear. Those uniforms have one identical shape or appearance.

[Misinformed.] Do you see that this is a variation of the word "inform"? We see the time machine[pg. vii] at the end, so we know it should be past tense. The prefix "mis-" means "bad." Think about misbehaving, behaving badly.

This word should mean "shaped the mind badly." Which is the best choice?

Write **misinformed** next to "shaped the mind in the wrong way, given bad information".

If you were told that the store was open late, but when you arrived it was closed, then you were misinformed. You were given bad information.

port

First, let's go through the words in the box, underlining the Latin root "port, to carry"

Now let's read all of the choices.

_____ door or gate, an entrance which carries to another place

_____ carried across

_____ point from which and to which things are carried by air

_____ carry over a distance instantaneously

_____ not carrying much weight or consequence

_____ carry across

[Teleport.] Look at the first word. The prefix is "tele-". Think of other words that use the prefix "tele-". Television, telephone. Both of those things allow you to see or hear something over a great distance instantaneously.

Which definition fits with that idea and "port, to carry"?

Write **teleport** next to "carry over a distance instantaneously."

This is an idea we see in science fiction, not real life. Star Trek characters can teleport or "beam me up" from a planet's surface to a ship in outer space instantaneously. Have you seen anything like this? One minute a person is on a planet, then it looks like swirling glitter, and then the person is gone, instantly transported back to the spaceship. We call this teleporting.

[Airport.] I think you already know what this means.

Write **airport** next to "point from which and to which things are carried by air".

Port means "to carry," and it also refers to a door or gate which things are carried through. The airport is like a gateway to the sky.

[Transport.] "Trans-" means "across." Port means "to carry."

Which definition fits? Pay attention to the present tense.

Write **transport** next to "carry across" (all the way at the bottom).

Trucks transport goods on the highways. They carry things across our country so that we can buy them.

[Transported.] There is a time machine [pg. vii] at the end of this word, so I know the definition should be past tense.

Write **transported** next to "carried across".

You may have tried to write transport here earlier. Pay attention to the clues that the parts of the word give you. The "-ed" is a clue that you have probably noticed before. It tells us when things are happening.

The Army brigade from Kansas transported its tanks by railroad and then a cargo ship when they went overseas.

[Unimportant.] Think of other words with the prefix "un-". Unhappy, unusual, unzip. "Un-" means "not".

Which definition fits with that idea? If you know what important means, you are simply looking for something that is "not important"

You might also notice the other parts of the word that give us clues about the meaning. Maybe you see "-ant" at the end and remember it changes words into nouns, either people who do something, or a thing associated with something. "Im-" is a variant of "in-" meaning "in, on, or toward" (the same prefix we saw in "inform"). Putting the pieces together we would have not+ toward + carry + (a thing that does this or is associated with this). Which is the best choice?

Write **unimportant** next to "not carrying much weight or consequence".

If something doesn't carry much weight or consequence, then it doesn't matter. It is not important.

[Portal.] The suffix "-al" is a naughty ending. It says /ul/. It means "relating to or characterized by." Often it turns a word into an adjective, a word that describes a thing, but the adjective can also be used as a noun in many cases. A last test at the end of a class is the final test, and it is called a final.

Port means "to carry," and it also refers to the gate or door through which things are carried. Does this fit with the definition we have left?

> Write **portal** next to "door or gate, an entrance which carries to another place".

Portal is another word for a door. It is often used in science fiction or fantasy to refer to a magical gateway.

rupt

Go through the words in the box, underlining the Latin root "rupt, to break or burst."

Let's read all of the choices.

_____ sudden change, unexpected, breaking the routine

_____ something that breaks something apart or causes disorder

_____ broke into the middle of something

_____ burst out

[Erupted.] The prefix for the first word is "e-". It is a variant of "ex-" which means "out." When I write this word, for some reason I always want to double the R, but that isn't how it is spelled! If I remember the morphemes, the parts of the word that have meaning like prefixes, roots, and suffixes, then I know that the prefix is "e-" and the root is "rupt". There is only one R because there is not an R in the prefix!

Notice the time machine at the end of this word [pg. vii].

Look for a definition that matches the meanings of "e-" and "rupt". It should be past tense.

Burst out. Burst is the same word in present and past tense. Today it burst. Yesterday it burst.

> Write **erupt** next to "burst out".

The volcano erupted 100 years ago, and liquid rock and ash burst out of the mountain.

[Abrupt.] The prefix "ab-" means "from or away" and rupt means "to burst."

This word is tricky and we will look at it more closely in the multiple choice section.

> For now, write **abrupt** next to "sudden change, unexpected, breaking the routine".

Our car made an abrupt change in direction when my dad swerved to avoid a deer.

[Interrupted.] "Inter-" means "between". Interstellar space is the space between stars.

I see a time machine at the end of this word [pg. vii]. The definition should be past tense.

We should have "between" plus "to break or burst," and it should be past tense. Which definition is the best choice?

> Write **interrupted** next to "broke into the middle of something".

I interrupted the conversation when I started talking while my mom was midsentence. [Disruption.] "Dis-" means "not, absence of, or apart." I dislike artichokes. I don't like them. Being at a distance means "we are apart."

So "dis-" could mean "not", or it could mean "apart". Does this word have something to do with not breaking or breaking apart?

I see "-tion", the naughty ending [pg. viii] that turns a word into a thing. This is the suffix "-ion", combined with the T from the root.

> Write **disruption** next to "something that breaks something apart or causes disorder".

The president had to tell the nation about an important event. There was a disruption during my favorite television show so that he could speak to the American people, and then it returned to the regularly scheduled program.

tract

Underline the roots you see in the words. "Tract, to pull."

Read all of the possible definitions.

_____ pulled toward

_____ able to be pulled away

_____ a vehicle used for pulling farm machinery

_____ to draw (pull) away, take away

_____ drawn out or lengthened (think of pulling the ending farther and farther forward), made longer

[Detract.] Look at the first word. "De-" means "down or away from." Think of defeat, defile, deport.

Do you see a definition that fits with "pull" and "down or away from"?

> Write **detract** next to "to draw (pull) away, take away".

Some ugly shoes may detract from the style of an outfit.

[Distractible.] We have encountered "dis-" again. It means "not, absence of, or apart."

I also see the suffix "-ible". The suffixes "-ible" and "-able" both mean "able." They mean "can do". This can be tricky if you are trying to spell a word. The suffix "-able" is more common, while "-ible" is used primarily with Latin roots. If you are trying to spell a word and you are not sure which one to use, use "able" unless you can find a Latin root in the word. With a Latin root, you should probably use "-ible".

This word should mean "not, absent, or apart" plus "able to pull." Can you choose the best definition?

>Write **distractible** next to "able to be pulled away".

If you are distractible, something more interesting may draw your attention. Your attention would not be with the original activity. Your attention would be absent. You may find that excited dogs are distractible. "Squirrel!"

[Attracted.] "At-" is a variation of "ad-" which means "to, toward, in, or near." Notice the time machine [pg. vii] at the end of the word.

>Can you piece the clues together? Which definition is the best fit?

>>Write **attracted** next to "pulled toward".

>The bug was attracted to the light. It seemed to be pulled toward the bug zapper.

[Protracted.] "Pro-" means "forward." Think of being propelled forward through the water with flippers. I see a time machine [pg. vii] on the end. The definition should be past tense.

>Which definition fits best?

>>Write **protracted** next to "drawn out or lengthened (think of pulling the ending farther and farther forward), made longer."

>Before the newspaper editor got her hands on the story, it was a bit protracted. She cut out the extra parts and made it shorter.

[Tractor.] The suffix "-or" means the same thing as "-er". It is "one who" or "that which." The "-or" is used with Latin roots, and "-er" is used with Anglo-Saxon base words (more common, everyday objects). If you recognize a Latin root in a word, you should use "-or". An actor acts. An elevator elevates (brings up). A tractor pulls. Can you find the best definition?

>Write **tractor** next to "a vehicle used for pulling farm machinery".

>Notice tractor is spelled OR, not ER, because "tract" is a Latin root.

Movement Review

Look at the pictures. Say the root that goes with the picture, do the movement, and say the meaning.

Write the root and the meaning next to the corresponding picture.

Lesson 1 Multiple Choice

Look at the next page. You have four selections. You can choose "I don't know" if none of the three other choice seem to fit, but a correct definition is there.

Detract. Do you see a Latin root in this word? If you see a Latin root in a word, you can underline it.

Tract is the root. What does it mean? [Do the movement, pretending to pull the rope] Tract, to pull.

I know it has something to do with pulling. You can look up what "de-" means in the prefix appendix in the back of this workbook. You could also think of other words with "de-" and see if that helps you figure out the meaning.

Deflate, demote, decompose, deplane.

"De-" means "down or away from."

"De-" means "down or away" and "tract" means "to pull," so "detract" should mean "to pull away."

When I look at this list of choices, I have to consider if any of them have anything to do with pulling away.

    C is the correct answer. Another way of saying "to pull away" is "to draw away"

Formation. Do you see a Latin root in this word?

If you see a Latin root in a word, you can underline it.

Form is the root. What does it mean? [Do the movement, pretending to push the gummy bear tummy back into shape] Form, to shape.

I know it has something to do with shape. This time there are suffixes at the end of this word.

I recognize the naughty ending "-tion" [pg. viii]. That naughty ending has two parts.

    The suffix "-ion" means "the act of, state of, or result of."

    The "t" is actually part of the other suffix in the word "ate." Bad Breath E [pg. vi] is dropped when you add "-ion." The suffix "-ate" means "cause or make."

    So "ation" means "to cause or make + the act of, state of, or result of."

    The only thing you really need to remember is that "-tion" (or in this case "ation") changes the word into a noun rather than a verb.

"Form" means "to shape" and "-ation" changes the root into a thing, so "formation" should mean "a thing that is shaped."

When I look at this list of choices, I have to consider if any of them have anything to do with shape.

    A- Military troops standing columns or squares are standing in shapes.

    B- I have heard of papers being called forms. Does this have anything to do with shape?

    C- If you are "for" something, you would vote yes. Does this have anything to do with shape?

        A is the correct answer. A military unit standing in lines is a formation.

You may have been tricked into choosing B because a document can be called a form. A document made with multiple copies containing blank spaces to be filled in is called a form because it refers to the "uniform" organization of the information. Uniform means "one shape," and so the document form is related to the Latin root "form." It might be an answer that you consider, but it is not the best choice. Remember that the Latin root "form" means "to shape," it doesn't mean "document."

The root in this word is "form," not "for" and so C doesn't make sense.

We can use formation in a sentence: The formation marched across the parade field as the band played.

Abrupt. Do you see a Latin root in this word?

If you see a Latin root in a word, you can underline it.

Rupt is the root. What does it mean? [Do the movement, fists in front of your face, bursting open] Rupt, to break or burst.

I know it has something to do with breaking or bursting. If you have a list of prefixes you can look up the prefix "ab-" or you can try to think of other words that start with that prefix.

Absent, absorb, abduct. "Ab-" means "from or away."

"Ab-" means "from or away" and "rupt" means "to break or burst," so "abrupt" should mean "to break away."

When I look at this list of choices, I have to consider if any of them have anything to do with breaking or bursting.

    A- I know people call their stomach muscles "abs." Does that have anything to do with breaking or bursting?

    B- A change could be a break in the routine, or breaking away. Bursting is sudden and possibly unexpected.

    C- I think I can eliminate this one. It doesn't have anything to do with breaking or bursting.

        B is the correct answer. A synonym for abrupt is sudden.

Think about a burst being sudden, and you will be able to remember that abrupt is sudden. Think of breaking the routine.

You may have been tricked into choosing A because abdominal muscles, the muscles around your torso, are referred to as "abs". Remember that in this case "ab-" means "from or away," and that we are looking for a definition that has to do with the Latin root "rupt."

Portfolio. Do you see a Latin root in this word?

If you see a Latin root in a word, you can underline it.

Port is the root. What does it mean? [Do the movement, bring your hands from one side to the other] Port, to carry.

I know it has something to do with carrying.

Foli is another root. It means "sheet or leaf." Can you think of other words with this root? Foliage, exfoliate.

☆ "Port" means "to carry," and "foli" means "sheet or leaf," so portfolio should mean something about carrying a sheet or leaf.

When I look at this list of choices, I have to consider if any of them have anything to do with carrying.

    A- I think I have heard of some sort of alcohol called port.

    B- A ship goes to a port.

    C- Port means "to carry," and foli means "sheet or leaf." I use sheets of paper.

    C is the correct answer. Portfolios are things used to carry sheets of paper. Often the papers are works of art or samples of your work.

You may have been tricked into choosing A because of port wine. Remember that in this case, port means "to carry."

B may have confused you because ships use ports, and they are called ports because of the Latin root "port." Ships carry good to and from ports. The best answer though, is C.

Lesson 2 Guide
scrib, script

First, let's go through the words in the box, underlining the Latin root "scrib, script, to write."

Now let's read all of the choices.

_____ an order written by a doctor before being given to a pharmacist, medication order

_____ written by hand, a handwritten book or document, or handwriting

_____ was able to write carelessly or meaninglessly

_____ to write underneath, to pledge, to agree

_____ writes beforehand, gives written directions

[Subscribe.] Look at the first word. Can you find the Latin root in it? Underline "scrib" which is part of "scrib, script, to write." The Bad Breath E [pg. vi] at the end is just for spelling.

"Sub-" is a prefix. Can you think of other words with this prefix? Submit, submerge, subtract. "Sub-" means "under, beneath, below, or secondary."

"Sub-" means "below," scribe means "to write." This word should mean "to write below." Which is the best choice?

> Write **subscribe** next to "to write underneath, to pledge, to agree."

Think of signing your name at the bottom of a contract. You would write your name below the words describing the agreement. Subscribe can refer to agreeing to pay for magazines that are sent to you, or just agreeing with an idea.

[Manuscript.] Look at the next word. Underline the root. "Manu-" is the prefix. If you know any Spanish, you may be able to figure out what this means. Spanish is also based on Latin.

Mano /mah nO/ is Spanish for hand. The Latin prefix "manu-" means "by hand."

"Manu-" means 'by hand," and "script" is part of "scrib, script, to write." This word should mean "to write by hand." Which is the best choice?

> Write **manuscript** next to "written by hand, a handwritten book or document, or handwriting."

Manuscript can refer to someone's handwriting, or a book or document that was written by hand instead of printed with a machine. It is also used to describe an author's story that is submitted to a publisher. These stories used to be handwritten by the author and then printed by the publisher. Now authors type their stories, but we still call them manuscripts.

[Prescription.] Find the root. "Script" is part of "scrib, script, to write." The prefix is "pre-" which means "before."

95

The suffix is "-ion". If you were dissecting the word to read it, you would see the Naughty Ending "-tion" [pg. viii]. Remember that the root indicates which Naughty Ending to use. The T in "script" means we should use "-tion." This suffix turns the word into a thing.

This word should mean "a thing" that is "written" "before".

There are two definitions listed here that are very similar. Look for the one referring to a thing.

> Write **prescription** next to "an order written by a doctor before being given to a pharmacist, medication order."

This word can be tricky to spell, but when you understand how the morphemes fit together, it will be easier to remember.

People say this word /per scrip shun/. The prefix "per-" [spell out P-E-R] means "through or completely." The prefix "pre" [spell out P-R-E] means "before."

A prescription is a note the doctor writes <u>before</u> you get your medicine, so you must use "P-R-E" even though people tend to say /per/.

☆

[Prescribes.] Underline the root. "Scrib" is part of "scrib, script, to write." The prefix is "pre-" meaning "before."

The Bad Breath E [pg. vi] is used here to change what the "i" says in scrib. The "-s" at the end of the verb indicates third person (he, she, it) singular (not they) is performing the verb. If the "-s" was not there, the Bad Breath E would be more obvious.

Which definition means "he, she, or it writes" "before"?

> Write **prescribes** next to "writes beforehand, gives written directions."

A doctor prescribes medicine, and then you get it from the pharmacist. Prescribes does not always mean something was actually written down. It may be used just as a recommendation for your benefit. A coach prescribes a good night of sleep before a competition.

☆

[Scribbled.] Underline the root. "Scrib" is part of "scrib, script, to write."

Notice the "L-" with another consonant in front of it. These guys have a gas mask [pg. vii]. They are willing to hug Bad Breath E and give him his own syllable. The suffix "-ble" is a variant of the suffix "ible" and it means "able, capable of." There is a time machine at the end of this word. If you add "-ed" to a word that ends with an "e," then you drop an "e". The time machine syllable fuses with the gas mask syllable.

We are looking for a definition that is past tense, "able to write." Which one fits?

> Write **scribbled** next to "was able to write carelessly or meaninglessly".

Scribbled is always used to refer to careless writing even though the parts of the word don't mention careless. Scribbled refers to fast, messy writing.

spec, spect, spic

First, let's go through the words in the box, underlining the Latin root "spec, spect, spic, to see or sort."

Now let's read all of the choices.

_____   easily seen or noticed, attracting special attention

_____   able to be looked down on, despised

_____   a kind or type

_____   to look back in thought, contemplate the past

_____   causing to look at through a point of view

_____   one who looks into carefully, examines

[Perspective.] Find the Latin root in the first word. "Spect" which is part of "spec, spect, spic, to see or sort." "Per-" is the prefix. It means "through or completely, thoroughly." Don't confuse it with "pre-". The suffix "-ive" means "causing or making."

This word should mean "cause to see completely, through, or thoroughly." Do any of the choices come close to that?

Write **perspective** next to "causing to look at through a point of view."

We might consider someone else's perspective if we think about how that person looks at a situation. Artists use perspective to make paintings look 3-D. They draw lines all leading to one point, and it looks like there is depth in the picture. It is as if you can look through the canvas and see into another world.

[Despicable.] Find the Latin root in the next word. "Spic" is part of "spec, spect, spic, to see or sort." "De-" is the prefix. It means "down or away from." Think of decay, defeat, deform.

The suffix is "-able." Usually "-ible" is used with Latin roots, but this word is an exception. If you would like to draw a time out chair under the A to help you remember it is breaking a rule, you can. [An "L" with two upside down "v"s for legs drawn under a part of the word that doesn't follow the rules can remind students of the anomaly.]

This word should mean "able to be looked down upon." Which choice is best?

Write **despicable** next to "able to be looked down on, despised."

Think of the movie *Despicable Me* and how the character wants to do bad, despicable things.

[Inspector.] Find the Latin root. "Spect" is part of "spec, spect, spic, to see or sort." The prefix "in-" can mean "in, on, or toward," or it can mean "not."

The suffix "-or" means the same thing as "-er." Both mean "one who," but "-or" is usually used with Latin roots.

This word should mean "one who looks into." The "in-" in this case means "into." Which is the best choice?

97

Write **inspector** next to "one who looks into carefully, examines."

An inspector is another word for detective.

[Retrospect.] Find the Latin root. "Spect" is part of "spec, spect, spic, to see or sort." The prefix is "retro-." You may have heard of clothes being retro. "Retro-" means "back." Retro clothes were in fashion a while back, or previously.

Which definition is the best fit?

Write **retrospect** next to "to look back in thought, contemplate the past".

In retrospect, the Titanic should have had more lifeboats.

[Conspicuous.] Find the Latin root. "Spic" is part of "spec, spect, spic, to see or sort." "Con-" means "together, with, joint, or jointly." It can also intensify a root. Spic means "see," so this can make it REALLY seen.

U is a letter sometimes used to connect Latin morphemes, and "-ous" (a Naughty Ending [pg. viii]) is a suffix that turns words into adjectives, words that describe things.

Conspicuous should be "a word that describes something that is really seen."

Which definition fits best?

Write **conspicuous** next to "easily seen or noticed, attracting special attention."

I felt rather conspicuous in my gym clothes when I walked into the fancy ballroom full of men in tuxedos and ladies in formal dresses.

[Species.] Find the Latin root. "Spec" is part of "spec, spect, spic, to see or sort."

The suffix "-ies" turns the root into a noun.

This word had its origins in the idea of seeing, but it began to be used as a kind. This word uses the alternate meaning of this root, "sort." Which is the best choice?

Write **species** next to "a kind or type."

All animals can be sorted into groups. The most specific group is the species. Animals can be called by a scientific name made up of their genus and species. These are ways of sorting living things so that into smaller and more specific groups. Grizzly bears can be called Ursus arctos, while the American black bear can be called Ursus americanus. Grizzly bears and American black bears are very similar; they are both animals, they both have backbones, they are mammals, and they are carnivores (they eat meat), and so they are in the same scientific groupings until they are sorted into species.

stru, struct, stry   flect, flex

Now we will look at words that contain one of two Latin roots. It is important to practice finding the roots when you don't know which one you are looking for.

First, let's go through the words in the box, underlining either the Latin root "stru, struct, stry, to build" or "flect, flex, to bend."

Now let's read all of the choices.

_____ change in pitch or tone of the voice, bend in the voice

_____ the act of pulling down, burning, making useless

_____ to build within, activity, systematic work, productive enterprises in a particular field

_____ to be turned or cast back, as light

_____ important, necessary, like a tool to build toward a goal

_____ an act of bending the knee in reverence

_____ to bend down, turn aside, turn from a true course

_____ the act of building by putting together parts

_____ to give meaning to, to pile up together

_____ not able to be bent

[Destruction.] Find the Latin root in the first word. I see "struct" which is part of "stru, struct, stry, to build."

The prefix is "de-" which means "down." Think of the word deflate. If you deflate a pool toy, you can imagine it collapsing down.

I see a Naughty Ending [pg. viii]. I know that this Naughty Ending is made up of the suffix "-ion" and uses the ending of the root to make "-tion." The Naughty Ending "-tion" turns the root into a thing.

This word should be "a thing" that has something to do with "building" and "down." Down is sort of the opposite of building. Do any of the choices fit with this idea?

Write **destruction** next to "the act of pulling down, burning, making useless."

The explosion resulted in the total destruction of the building.

[Inflection.] Find the Latin root. I see "flect" which is part of "flect, flex, to bend."

The prefix is "in-" which means "in, on, or toward," or it can mean "not."

I see the Naughty Ending [pg. viii] "-tion" made up of the suffix "-ion" and the last letter of the root. The Naughty Ending "-tion" turns the word into a thing.

This word should be "a thing that bends in, on, or toward."

Write **inflection** next to "change of pitch or tone of the voice, bend in the voice."

Using inflection when you read aloud makes the story interesting. You raise your voice at the end of a question and bring it down at the end of a sentence. If you do not use inflection in your voice, you sound like a robot, and you are hard to understand.

[Inflexible.] Underline the Latin root. "Flect" is part of "flect, flex, to bend." The prefix "in-" means "in, on, or toward," or it can mean "not."

The suffixes "-ible" and "-able" both mean "able." This word has a Latin root, so we spell it "I-B-L-E."

This word should mean "able to bend toward or not able to bend," depending on which meaning of the prefix is used. You can look the word up in a dictionary to see which one is the correct use of "in."

This time "in-" means "not."

Write **inflexible** next to "not able to be bent".

Inflexible can refer to an attitude or a physical quality. Someone who sticks to the rules without exception would be inflexible. A rigid beam that will not bend at all is also inflexible.

[Instrumental.] Underline the Latin root. "Stru" is part of "stru, struct, stry, to build." We have the prefix "in-" again! It means "towards" or it can mean "not."

There are two suffixes. The suffix "-ment" means "act of, state of, or result of." The suffix "-al" means "relating to or characterized by."

This word uses the first meaning of "in-," toward.

The word should mean "characterized by" "the act of" "building" "toward." Do any of the choices fit with those ideas? Think of a tool. A tool can be called an instrument. Something is instrumental if it is needed to achieve something.

Write **instrumental** next to "important, necessary, like a tool to build toward a goal."

The quarterback is instrumental in the success of the football team.

[Industry.] Underline the Latin root. This time, the root is at the end of the word. "Stry" is part of "stru, struct, stry, to build." The prefix "indu-" means "within."

This word should mean "to build" + "within."

Can you find the best definition?

Write **industry** next to "to build within, activity, systematic work, productive enterprises in a particular field."

The use of this word has changed a bit since its original meaning in Latin. Its literal meaning "to build within" referred to hard work, and it now means "a business, or type of business, that builds or produces things." The automobile industry makes cars. You can think of an industry as something that builds a product within its factories.

[Genuflection.] Underline the Latin root. "Flect" is part of "flect, flex, to bend." "Genu" means "knee."

The Naughty Ending "-tion" [pg. viii] is made up of the end of the Latin root and the suffix "-ion". It turns the word into a thing.

This word should mean "a thing that" "bends" "the knee." Which is the best choice?

Write **genuflection** next to "an act of bending the knee in reverence."

A marriage proposal in our culture typically requires a man's genuflection. Genuflection can also be used to refer to an attitude and not a body position. "He approached the king with genuflection."

[Construction.] Underline the Latin root. "Struct" is part of "stru, struct, stry, to build." "Con-" is the prefix that means "with or together."

The Naughty Ending "-tion" [pg. viii] is made up of the end of the root and the suffix "-ion," and it turns the word into a thing.

This word should mean "a thing that" "builds" "together." Which is the best choice?

Write **construction** next to "the act of building by putting together parts."

Construction workers build a house.

[Reflect.] Underline the Latin root. "Flect" is part of "flect, flex, to bend." "Re-" is the prefix. It means "back or again."

This word should mean "to bend" "back." Are there any similar definitions listed?

Write **reflect** next to "to be turned or cast back, as light."

A mirror can reflect your image by bending bend back or bouncing back the light waves that your eye translates into a picture. You can also reflect on the past by thinking about something that happened before. You would bend your thoughts back. "The old man reflected about his time as a boy and wished that some things had gone differently." "The shiny metal reflects light."

[Construe.] Underline the Latin root. "Stru" is part of "stru, struct, stry, to build." The Bad Breath E [pg. vi] at the end of the root is there for spelling, not meaning. The prefix "con-" means "with or together."

This word should mean "to build" "together." Which is the best fit?

Write **construe** next to "to give meaning to, to pile up together."

Construe refers to building meaning, not physically building with your hands. If you gather bits of information, then you would pile them up to form an understanding. You could use the word "understand" in place of the word "construe." "No one could construe her actions as dishonest. No one could understand her actions as dishonest."

[Deflect.] Underline the Latin root. "Flect" is part of "flect, flex, to bend." "De-" means "down or away from."

This word should mean "to bend" "down or away from." Does this fit with the last blank?

Write **deflect** next to "to bend down, turn aside, turn from a true course."

Usually deflect is used when describing a response to a question. If a reporter asks a politician an uncomfortable question, the politician may deflect the question by changing the subject. The politician may turn the discussion down a different path in order to avoid talking about something that is uncomfortable.

Movements Review

Look at the pictures. Say the root that goes with the picture, do the movement, and say the meaning.

Write the root and the meaning next to the corresponding picture.

Lesson 2 Multiple Choice

These words all have Latin Roots.

We have eight Latin roots listed at the top. Underline the root that you see in the word.

Use the movement to help you remember what the root means, and find that meaning in one of the choices below the word.

Circumflex. Underline the Latin root. "Flex" is part of "flect, flex, to bend." Read each choice. Do any of the choices have to do with bending?

If you are still stuck, you could look for other clues. Do you know of any words that start with "circum"? That might help you make an educated guess about which answer is the best choice.

We can always go to the dictionary for more information.

Circumflex. A) winding around, a vowel under a bent mark.

You find circumflex vowels in many foreign languages. Have you seen funny bent marks over letters in foreign words?

Uniformity. Underline the Latin root. "Form, to shape." Read each choice. Do any of the choices have to do with shape?

The word gives me more clues. Do you recognize the prefix "uni-"? Can you think of other words with that prefix that might help you guess its meaning?

Can you take off the suffix at the end of this word? Do you know what "uniform" means?

Uniformity. C) overall same shape, homogeneity, or regularity.

"He cut the pieces of wood with such uniformity, that the fence looked professionally made."

Restructure. Underline the Latin root. "Struct" is part of "stru, struct, stry, to build." Read each choice. Do any of the choices have to do with building?

Do you know what the prefix means? Does that help?

Restructure. B) to change the mode of building or parts.

"Our fort kept collapsing, and we decided to restructure the main wall. We replaced the couch cushions with chairs."

Support. Underline the Latin root. "Port, to carry." Read each choice. Do any of them have to do with carrying?

Support. B) to bear, hold up, carry the weight.

"I was able to get through a difficult time thanks to the support of my family." Support can be physically carrying the weight like a column in a building, it can be emotionally carrying the weight like hugging someone when they are crying, or it can be financially carrying the weight by paying all of the bills.

Traction. Underline the Latin root. "Tract, to pull." Read each choice. Do any of the choices have to do with pulling?

Traction. C) the act of pulling, a sticking force.

There are two common ways we use the word traction.

"My sneakers couldn't get any traction on the slippery floor."

"After the terrible car accident, he had to be put in traction in the hospital. There were clamps, braces, and wires everywhere, pulling his body back into the proper shape."

Suspicion. Underline the Latin root. "Spic" is part of "spec, spect, spic, to see, sort." Read each choice. Do any of the choices have to do with seeing or sorting?

Do you know any other words that are similar that might use another form of the same root? [Suspect.]

Can you guess what the prefix means based on other words you know? Suspend, suspect... (it is a variant of sub...submerge, submit.) It means "under."

Suspicion. B) a doubt, a reason to look at carefully.

"I have a suspicion that I am getting sick."

Corruptible. Underline the Latin root. "Rupt, to break or burst." Read each choice. Do any of them have to do with breaking or bursting?

Corruptible. A) able to be destroyed, morally breakable.

"We learned that the politician was corruptible after all when it was revealed that she had taken bribes."

Inscribe. Underline the Latin root. "Scrib" is part of "scrib, script, to write." Read each choice. Do any of them have to do with writing?

Inscribe. C) to write in or on.

"I bought a special book for my mom and decided to inscribe a message on the inside cover about how much I love her."

Special. Underline the Latin root. "Spec" is part of "spec, spect, spic, to see, sort." Read each choice. Do any of them have to do with seeing or sorting?

Do you already know what this word means?

    Special. A) different from what is ordinary, particular kind.

"My grandma says I'm special." "I have a special toothbrush that plays music while I brush my teeth."

Performance. Underline the Latin root. "Form, to shape." Read each choice. Do any of the choices have to do with shape?

What is the prefix. Is it "pre-, before" or "per-, through or completely"?

If you take off the suffix do you know this word?

    Performance. C) a thing that provides shape to an idea or character.

"The actor's performance was outstanding." Sometimes this word is mispronounced and that makes it difficult to spell. Remember that this is a "complete shape", not a "before shape", and so this word is spelled "P-E-R," not "P-R-E."

Lesson 3 Guide
dic, dict

First, let's go through the words in the box, underlining the Latin root "dic, dict, to say."

Now let's read all of the choices.

_____ to declare or tell in advance; prophesy; foretell

_____ to give up or renounce; proclaim away; say you don't want it

_____ to speak the contrary or opposite of

_____ a decree issued by authority; proclamation sent out to subjects

_____ declare what is true; judgment; decision

[Contradict.] "Dict" is part of "dic, dict, to say." "Contra-" is a prefix. Can you think of other words that are similar to contra? Contrary, contrast, contraband. It means "against, opposite, contrasting."

This word should mean "to speak against." Do any of the choices fit with this?

> Write **contradict** next to "to speak the contrary or opposite of."

You might contradict your teacher if she says something you disagree with. You might contradict yourself if you say you believe something and then say you don't believe it.

[Predict.] Look at the next word. Did you find the root? "Dict" is part of "dic, dict, to say."

The prefix is "pre-." Can you think of other words with "pre-"? Preview, prepare, pretest, prefix. "Pre-" means "before or earlier."

This word should mean "to speak before." Which choice is best?

> Write **predict** next to "to declare or tell in advance; prophesy; foretell."

On February 2, people try to predict what will happen with the weather by watching a groundhog.

[Verdict.] What is the root? "Dict" is part of "dic, dict, to say."

This word is actually composed of two roots. "Ver or veri" are forms of the same root. Can you think of other words with "ver" or "veri?" Very, verify. "Ver" means "true and genuine."

This word should mean to "speak truth." Do any of the definitions seem like a good choice?

> Write **verdict** next to "declare what is true; judgment; decision."

You may be familiar with this word if you have learned anything about trials or courtrooms. The verdict is the decision from a judge or jury. The verdict is either "guilty" or "not guilty."

[Abdicate.] Did you find the root? "Dic" is part of "dic, dict, to say."

The prefix is "ab-." Can you think of other words with "ab-"? Abrupt, absorb, abstain. "Ab-" means "from or away."

The suffix is "-ate." It changes a word into a verb that causes or makes something an action, or it changes it to a describing word.

This word should mean "causing something to go away by speaking." Which definitions matches this?

Write **abdicate** next to "to give up or renounce; proclaim away; say you don't want it."

If a prince doesn't want to be the king, he would abdicate his throne.

[Edict.] What is the root? "Dict" is part of "dic, dict, to say."

The prefix is "e-." Can you think of other words that might use this prefix? Eject, erupt, evaporate, evacuate. "E-" is a variant of "ex-" and it means "out."

This word should mean "to speak out." Does that fit with the last definition left?

Write **edict** next to "a decree issued by authority; proclamation sent out to subjects."

A king would issue an edict if he wants his subjects to know about a new rule he has made.

fer

Look at the words in the box. Underline the Latin root "fer, to bear or yield."

Read all of the choices.

_____	one who carries others back to a source of information in order to make a decision or ruling; judge
_____	bearing, producing, or capable of bearing crops or offspring
_____	to bear under; undergo or feel pain or distress
_____	the outer boundary of a circle; the path born around a point
_____	to present for acceptance or rejection; to carry to, to bring
_____	to carry across; move from one place or person to another

[Circumference.] Look at the first word. Did you find the root? "Fer, to bear or yield."

"Circum-" is the prefix. Can you think of other words with this prefix? Circumvent, circumstance, circumcise. "Circum-" means "around." This prefix usually has something to do with a circle.

The suffix is "-ence." This is a Good Vowel Naughty Ending [pg. viii]. It means "action, state, or quality." It turns the root into a thing.

This word should mean "a thing" + "bear" +" around (maybe a circle)." Do any of the definitions have to do with carrying around or circles?

> Write **circumference** next to "the outer boundary of a circle; the path born around a point."

Have you heard of Pi Day? It is celebrated every year on March 14 (3/14). Pi is a number used in math. It never ends or repeats. It just keeps going and going. People like to celebrate Pi day by eating pie. Where do we get this funny number? It is the ratio of the circumference (the distance around the edge of a circle) to the diameter (the distance across a circle). It is 3.14159265... The circumference is the length around a circle.

[Fertile.] Did you find the Latin root? "Fer, to bear or yield."

The suffix is "–ile" which means "relating to, suited for, or capable of." What should we do with the "T?" You could include the "T" with the root. This word has the Latin root "fer," but it developed from the Latin word "fertilis." Perhaps the T is a remnant of that word.

This word should mean "relating to, suited for, or capable of bearing." Which definition is best?

> Write **fertile** next to "bearing, producing, or capable of bearing crops or offspring."

Fertile soil is soil with lots of nutrients that will yield a lot of crops.

[Referee.] Did you find the Latin root? "Fer, to bear or yield."

"Re-" is the prefix. Can you think of other words with this prefix? Recall, refresh, reject. "Re-" means" back or again."

The suffix is "-ee." It means "one who receives the action." It changes the word into a person.

This word should mean "one who carries back." Do any of the choices match this?

You may have heard this word in sports.

> Write **referee** next to "one who carries others back to a source of information in order to make a decision or ruling; judge."

The referee understands the rules, and when there is a disagreement in a game, the referee will make a decision based on the rules. He will go back to the rulebook. "The referee threw a penalty flag on the field."

[Transfer.] Did you find the Latin root? "Fer, to bear or yield."

The prefix is "trans-." Transport, transmit, transpose. "Trans-" means "across or beyond."

This word should mean "bear across." Which is the best choice?

> Write **transfer** next to "to carry across; move from one place or person to another."

You can be transferred to a new office, or you can transfer your line leader responsibility to another person.

[Offer.] Did you find the Latin root? "Fer, to bear or yield."

"Of-" is the prefix. It is a variant of the prefix "ob-". When it is used before a root that starts with F, "of-" is used. It means "down, against, or facing." It can also mean "to."

This word should mean "to bear to." Which is the best choice?

Write **offer** next to "to present for acceptance or rejection; to carry to, to bring."

"I offer my friend a bite of my apple."

[Suffer.] Did you underline the Latin root? "Fer, to bear or yield."

"Suf-" is the prefix. It is a variant of the prefix "sub-". When it is used before words beginning with F, "suf-" is used. It means "under, beneath, below, or secondary."

This word should mean "to bear under." Does that match the last definition we have left?

Write **suffer** next to "to bear under; undergo or feel pain or distress."

"Some peasants suffered from disease and hunger in the Middle Ages."

mit, miss   duc, duce, duct

Now we will look at words that contain one of two Latin roots. It is important to practice finding the roots when you don't know which one you are looking for.

Look at the words in the box. Underline the Latin root "mit, miss, to send" or "duc, duce, duct, to lead."

Let's read all of the possible definitions.

_____ one who is sent out, a representative sent on a mission

_____ the state of being brought back, lowered in rank, lessened

_____ to lead in, bring in; present to another so as to make acquainted

_____ put under; let go of power and send it to another

_____ carry off or lead away, kidnap

_____ to send through, allow

_____ to send out, discharge, release

_____ to lead out of ignorance, make qualified

_____ to send to join together, pledge, promise

_____ to lead or bring together; management of others or self

[Permit.] Did you find the Latin root in the first word? I see "mit" which is part of "mit, miss, to send or let go." ☆

The prefix is "per-" which means "through or completely, thoroughly."

This word should mean "to send or let go through." Which is the best choice?

    Write **permit** next to "to send through, allow."

"The teacher will permit the student to go to the restroom." Think of guards at a castle who permit you to go through the gate. They send you through.

[Introduce.] I see the Latin root "duce" which is part of "duc, duce, duct, to lead." ☆

The prefix is "intro-" which means "in or inward."

This word should mean "to lead in." Which is the best choice?

    Write **introduce** next to "to lead in, bring in; present to another so as to make acquainted."

"I will introduce my new friend to my mother."

[Reduction.] Which root did you find? I see "duct" which is part of "duc, duce, duct, to lead." ☆

The prefix is "re-" which means "back or again." I see the Naughty Ending "–tion" [pg. viii]. I know that the Naughty Endings are usually composed of the last letter of a root and a suffix. The suffix is "–ion." I remember that "–tion" makes the word into a thing.

This word should mean "a thing that is lead back." Which is the best choice?

    Write **reduction** next to "the state of being brought back, lowered in rank, lessened."

Reduction can be used when we talk about buying something on sale. "The reductions taken at the register lessen the price."

Reduction can be used to refer to a punishment in the military. "After his bad behavior, the specialist had a reduction in rank." He was back to being a private.

Reduction can be used in cooking. Boiling a liquid so that the water evaporates is how you make a reduction, a condensed cooking liquid.

[Commit.] Which Latin root did you underline? I see "mit" part of "mit, miss, to send." ☆

The prefix is "com-." It is a variant of "con-" and is used before roots beginning with M. "Com-" means "together, with, jointly."

This word should mean "to send together, with, jointly." Which is the best choice?

    Write **commit** next to "to send to join together, pledge, promise."

Will you commit to working hard? Do you promise to do your best? Leaders commit military troops. They send them to work together with other militaries to fight a problem.

[Educate.] Which Latin root did you find? I see "duc" which is part of "duc, duce, duct, to lead." ☆

The prefix "e-" is a variant of "ex-" and they both mean "out."

The suffix is "-ate," and it means "cause or make." It changes a word into a verb, an action word, or an adjective, a word that describes a thing.

This word should mean "cause to lead out." Which definition is best?

> Write **educate** next to "to lead out of ignorance, make qualified."

When a teacher educates you, she leads you out of a dark place where you don't understand into a bright place full of knowledge.

[Emissary.] Which Latin root did you find? I see "miss" which is part of "mit, miss, to send." ☆

The prefix is "e-" (we just had this one... the variant of "ex-") which means "out."

The suffix is "-ary." It means "relating to, place where." It can change a word into a noun or an adjective.

This word should mean "something that is sent out." Which definition is best?

> Write **emissary** next to "one who is sent out, a representative sent on a mission."

"The king sent an emissary since he was unable to travel."

[Conduct.] Which Latin root did you find? I see "duct" which is part of "duc, duce, duct, to lead." ☆

This word can be pronounced two ways. When the emphasis is placed on the first syllable, it is pronounced /con/, but when the emphasis is placed on the last syllable, the first is pronounced /cun/.

The prefix is "con-" which means "together, with, jointly."

This word should mean something like "to lead together." Do any of the definitions fit?

> Write **conduct** next to "to lead or bring together; management of others or self."

The way in which you /cun/ conduct yourself is the way in which you behave.

You would /cun/ conduct an orchestra by leading the instrumentalists, telling them when to start and stop, and how to play together.

Your /con/ conduct (spelled the same, pronounced differently) is your behavior. This word in all three uses has to do with management or leadership.

[Emit.] Did you find the Latin root? I see "mit" which is part of "mit, miss, to send." ☆

The prefix is "e-" which is a variant of "ex-" and means "out."

This word should mean "to send out." Do any of the definitions match that idea?

> Write **emit** next to "to send out, discharge, release."

An LED stands for a light emitting diode. It sends out light.

[Submit.] Did you find the Latin root? I see "mit" which is part of "mit, miss, to send or let go."

The prefix is "sub-" which means "under, beneath, or secondary." Think of a submarine, subtract, submit, or a substitute.

This word should mean "to send under." Which is the best choice?

> Write **submit** next to "put under; let go of power and send it to another."

You would submit to the authority of a king. When you submit to your parents' guidance, you put yourself beneath their authority. This word usually describes putting yourself underneath the one who makes the rules, not a physical position, although you may show that you have submitted by bowing.

[Abduct.] Which Latin root did you find? I see "duct" which is part of "duc, duce, duct, to lead."

The prefix is "ab-" which means "from or away." Think of absorb or absent.

This word should mean" to lead away." Does that fit with the last definition left?

> Write **abduct** next to "carry off or lead away, kidnap."

"A bad guy may try to abduct or kidnap someone."

Movements Review

Look at the pictures. Say the root that goes with the picture, do the movement, and say the meaning.

Write the root and the meaning below the corresponding picture.

Lesson 3 Multiple Choice

These words all have Latin Roots.

We have twelve Latin roots listed at the top. Underline the root that you see in the word. Use the movement to help you remember what the root means, and find that meaning in one of the choices below the word.

Confer. Underline the Latin root. "Fer, to bear or yield." Read each choice. Do any of the choices have to do with bearing or yielding?

If you are still stuck, you could look for other clues. Do you know of any words that start with "con-"? That might help you make an educated guess about which answer is the best choice. Convert, concur. If you know Spanish, you might know the meaning of this prefix. It means "together."

> **Confer. C) gather together, compare, bring together.**

If you are playing a trivia game with teams, you would confer with your teammates before answering a question. You might be familiar with a word that uses the same prefix and root: conference. A parent/teacher conference is an event where a parent and teacher get together to talk about a student.

Inspector. Underline the Latin root. "Spect" is part of "spec, spect, spic, to see, sort." Read each choice. Do any of the choices have to do with seeing or sorting?

The word gives me more clues. Do you recognize the prefix "in-"? Can you think of other words with that prefix that might help you guess its meaning?

Do you recognize the suffix "-or"?

  Inspector. A) one who looks into carefully, examines.

Have you heard of the movie or cartoon "Inspector Gadget"? Inspector Gadget is a detective. He looks into things. He searches for clues.

Ductile. Underline the Latin root. "Duct" is part of "duc, duce, duct, to lead." Read each choice. Do any of the choices have to do with leadership?

Maybe you can eliminate some of the choices. Does "duct" have anything to do with the sense of touch? Does being "drawn out" have to do with being led? If you still aren't sure, you can use a dictionary.

  Ductile. B) capable of being drawn out into wires or threads.

Metals like gold are ductile. They can be pulled into thin strips instead of breaking. They are able to be led into a new shape.

Postscript. Underline the Latin root. "Script" is part of "scrib, script, to write." Read each choice. Do any of the choices have to do with writing?

The word gives me more clues. Do you recognize the prefix "post-"? Can you think of other words with that prefix that might help you guess its meaning? Postmark, postpone. "Post-" means "after."

  Postscript. B) additional phrase after the conclusion of a letter.

You are probably familiar with the abbreviation for this word. When you want to write something else after you have signed your name on a note or letter, you write P.S. P.S. is short for postscript.

Indicate. Underline the Latin root. "Dic" is part of "dic, dict, to say." Read each choice. Do any of the choices have to do with speaking?

Maybe you can eliminate some of the choices. If you still aren't sure, you can use a dictionary.

  Indicate. A) be a sign of, show, make known.

If you like math and art, those interests may indicate a future job in engineering. To indicate means "to tell."

Omit. Underline the Latin root. "mit" is part of "mit, miss, to send or let go." Read each choice. Do any of the choices have to do with sending?

The word gives me more clues. The prefix "o-" is a variation of "ob-" which means "away, against, to." "O-" is used before roots that start with M.

Omit. C) fail to do, make, use, send; leave out.

If you have to shorten a story that you are writing, you might omit a paragraph. You would send away the paragraph or kick it out of your paper. You would leave it out.

Infrastructure. Underline the Latin root. "Struct" is part of "stru, struct, stry, to build." Read each choice. Do any of the choices have to do with building?

Infrastructure. A) built below a system or organization, framework.

Infrastructure is anything that is built to support something else. Roads and pipes are infrastructure for a city. The building and office desks might be infrastructure for a business.

Abstract. Underline the Latin root. "Tract, to pull." Read each choice. Do any of the choices have to do with pulling?

The word gives me more clues. The prefix "ab-" means "from or away."

Abstract. C) withdrawn or separated from material objects.

Abstract art doesn't depict material objects. It uses color and line to depict emotion. It is pulled away from the physical, toward the emotional.

Deport. Underline the Latin root. "Port, to carry." Read each choice. Do any of the choices have to do with carrying?

Deport. B) to send or carry off.

If someone visiting from another country commits a crime, the government may deport them, or send them away.

Intermittent. Underline the Latin root. "Mit" is part of "mit, miss, to send or let go." Read each choice. Do any of the choices have to do with sending?

Intermittent. C) alternately sending and not sending.

The intermittent lighting is a distraction. I can sometimes see things, and then it is too dark to see. Perhaps a wire is loose. Maybe the electricity is sent through the circuit, and then the circuit is broken.

Lesson 4 Guide
cred

Underline the Latin root in each word in the box.

Use the clues that the prefixes or suffixes give you, or use a dictionary, to match the word to the definition below. Write the word next to the definition. Please read all of the choices before deciding which one is the best match.

_____ something that brings belief to; certification; authority

_____ so extraordinary that it is believed to be impossible

_____ "I believe," a formula of beliefs

_____ not believing, skeptical

_____ trust something will be cared for, paid back; acknowledge, honor

[Credit.] Look at the first word. Can you find the Latin root in it? Underline "cred, to believe."

What is the "-it" at the end? Is it a suffix? In this case, it is not. The "it is from the original Latin language. Just like in Spanish, the verbs were conjugated, meaning, their endings were changed to indicate who was doing the action and when the action was done. In this case the "it" is left over from a conjugation meaning "a neutral party believed in the past."

Credit should mean "someone believed." Which answer is the best choice?

> Write **credit** next to "trust something will be cared for, paid back; acknowledge, honor."

If someone is believed in, then they may be trusted with something, or they have proven themselves.

Credit can refer to a place in the community, a status, or honor. We give someone credit for doing a good job. Credit can mean "acknowledge." We believe in them.

It can also be used to indicate a belief that someone will pay for something in the future. Your parents may use credit to make a large purchase. The store or creditor believes your parents will pay the full amount in increments in the future.

[Incredible.] Underline the Latin root. "Cred, to believe."

I see the prefix "in-" which means "not." Inactive, indirect, insane.

I see the suffix "-ible" which means "able." Remember that most of the time, if you see the suffix "-ible" it means there is a Latin root in the word. The suffix "-able" could be used with any root morpheme, but most of the time, it is not a Latin root. The suffixes "-ible" and "-able" both mean the same thing.

This word should mean "not believable." Which is the best choice?

Write **incredible** next to "so extraordinary that it is believed to be impossible."

The Incredibles are super heroes that have amazing abilities. What they do seems impossible (and in reality it is). Their strength, flexibility, invisibility, and speed are all so amazing that even if you saw them, you could not believe they were doing what they were doing.

[Accreditation.] Underline the Latin root. In this case, we can underline credit, which is just the past tense ☆ of "cred, to believe."

I see the prefix "ac-" which is a variant of "ad-", meaning "to, toward, in, or near." "Ac-" is used before words beginning with C, K, or QU. Accept, acknowledge, acquit.

I see "-ation" at the end of the word. The suffix "-ation" = "-ate" + "-ion." We drop the Bad Breath E [pg. vi] when we combine the two suffixes. The suffix "-ate" means "to cause or make" and "-ion" means "act of, state of, or result of." It makes a word a thing. Adding "-ion" changes the word into a noun.

This word should mean "something that makes or causes toward being believed." Which is the best choice?

Write **accreditation** next to "something that brings belief to; certification; authority."

It is important that you attend a college with accreditation. That means the college has gone through a certification process. The college has a proven, believable result. It has been certified.

[Incredulous.] Underline the Latin root. "Cred, to believe."

I see the prefix "in-" again. Do you remember what it means? It means "not."

I see "-ulous" at the end. Do you recognize the Naughty Ending [pg. viii] "ous"? It is pronounced /us/, not /ows/. The suffix "-ulous" means "a quality or a tendency."

This word should mean "a tendency to not believe." Which answer is the best choice?

Write **incredulous** next to "not believing, skeptical."

"I felt rather incredulous when the man told me he had been a movie star as a child."

[Credo.] Underline the Latin root. "Cred, to believe."

The "o" at the end of this word is also left over from conjugating the Latin verb. The Spanish verb *hablar* means "to speak." If you want to say, "I speak," then you change the ending. *Hablar* becomes *hablo*. The same thing happened in Latin. The "o" is left over from making the Latin verb "to believe" into "I believe".

This word should mean "I believe." Which is the best choice?

Write **credo** next "'I believe,' a formula of beliefs."

The word credo is the first word in a famous set of beliefs that some people would say in church called the Apostles' Creed. It means, "I believe," and over time, "credo" came to be used as the term for any set of beliefs, even those not associated with a church.

vert, vers

Underline the Latin root in each word in the box. "Vert, vers, to turn."

Use the clues that the prefixes or suffixes give you, or use a dictionary, to match the word to the definition below. Write the word next to the definition. Please read all of the choices before deciding which one is the best match.

_____ to turn a phrase with another, talk

_____ different, turned apart, a wide range

_____ turned up to the highest point overhead, straight up and down

_____ turn from underneath, overthrow, destroy

_____ capable of turning from one task to another, having many uses

[Converse.] Look at the first word. Can you find the Latin root in it? Underline "vers", which is part of "vert, vers, to turn."

The "e" at the end of the word is just there for spelling. It doesn't have a meaning. Words tend to end "-ss" or "-se," otherwise we might think the "-s" at the end meant more than one.

I see the prefix "con-". Do you remember what it means? "Con-" means "together."

This word should mean "to turn together." Which answer is the best choice?

Write **converse** next to "to turn a phrase with another, talk."

Sometimes language can be referred to as a verse. Think of a line of poetry or a song. Think of how your inflection goes up and down. Now think of your voice curving up and down, and then your friend's voice curving up and down. To converse means "to speak with someone." Your voices curve or turn together.

[Subvert.] Underline the Latin root, "vert" which is part of "vert, vers, to turn."

I see the prefix "sub-" which means "under, beneath, below, or secondary."

This word should have something to do with turning and under.

Write **subvert** next to "turn from underneath, overthrow, destroy."

Think of unhappy peasants who do not wish to be subject to the evil king's rule any more. They would rise up and subvert his rule. They would overturn his throne.

[Versatile.] Underline the Latin root, "vers" which is part of "vert, vers, to turn."

I see "-atile" at the end. This is made up of two suffixes, "-ate" and "-ile." We drop the Bad Breath E [pg. vi] in "-ate" when we add "-ile" to the end. The suffix "-ate" means "to cause or make," and "-ile" means "related to, suited for, or capable of."

This word should mean "made capable of turning." Which answer is the best choice?

Write **versatile** next to "capable of turning from one task to another, having many uses."

Something is versatile if you can use it for more than one purpose. A stool is versatile. You can stand on it, you can sit on it, or you can use it as an end table and put your drink on it. Think of turning from one task to the next.

[Vertical.] Underline the Latin root, "vert" which is part of "vert, vers, to turn."

I see "-ical" at the end. The "-ic," in this case, is a suffix that turns a verb into a noun. The Naughty Ending [pg. viii] "-al" is also suffix. It means "relating to or characterized by." It changes the noun into an adjective.

This word should mean "relating to or characterized by a thing that turns."

Write **vertical** next to "turned up to the highest point overhead, straight up and down."

In this case, the thing that turns is called a vertex. A vertex is the highest point. When you throw a ball up in the air, it curves up, and then it curves back down. The highest point on that curve is the vertex. Vertical meant "turned up to the vertex." That is a very complicated way of saying straight up and down. If you are standing up instead of lying down, then your body is vertical.

[Diverse.] Underline the Latin root, "vers" which is part of "vert, vers, to turn."

Notice the Bad Breath E [pg. vi] again. It is just there for spelling. Words end" -ss" or "-se." If they didn't, we might think the word meant more than one.

The prefix is "di-" which is a variant of "dis-" meaning apart. "Di-" is used before roots that begin with *b, d, l, m, n, r, s, v,* and sometimes *g* and *j.* It is quite common.

This word should mean "turn apart." Which answer is the best choice?

Write **diverse** next to "different, turned apart, a wide range."

Think of a rainbow. Light is bent or turned, and the light waves are spread apart so that you can see all of the different colors. Diverse usually means you have a group of different things. Your crayons are a diverse collection of colors. The zoo has a diverse display of animals.

pel, puls   fac, fact, fect, fic

We are going to look at words that contain one of two Latin roots. Each of these roots has multiple forms. You may find it helpful to say all of the forms, do the movement, and say the meaning after you underline a root.

Underline the Latin root in each word in the box. These words will include the roots "pel, puls, to push" and "fac, fact, fect, fic, to make or do."

Use the clues that the prefixes or suffixes give you, or use a dictionary, to match the word to the definition below. Write the word next to the definition. Please read all of the choices before deciding which one is the best match.

_____ pushed from within, swayed by emotions, rash

_____ something that is made up, imaginary

_____ to drive in various directions, to push away, disperse

_____ the state of being pushed away, driven back, disgusted

_____ a well to-do person who makes things easier, supporter, patron

_____ throb, beat, to push blood through vessels

_____ to make or do inside of something, taint, spread impurity in

_____ having made up to the needed amount; adequate, enough

_____ to make easier, less difficult; cause to be doable

_____ to drive together (cattle), force (people)

[Dispel.] Look at the first word. Can you find the Latin root in it? Underline "pel" which is part of "pel, puls, to push."

I see the prefix "dis-" which means "not, absence of, or apart."

This word should mean " push apart or push an absence of." Which answer is the best choice?

Write **dispel** next to "to drive in various directions, to push away, disperse."

If someone reassures you by telling you that you can do something, that person would "dispel any doubts" from your mind. The doubts would be pushed out so that they are no longer there. The doubts are absent.

[Infect.] Underline the Latin root, "fect" which is part of "fac, fact, fect, fic, to make or do."

I see the prefix "in-" which means "in, on, or toward."

This word should mean "to make or do something" combined with "in, on, or toward." Which answer is best?

Write **infect** next to "to make or do inside of something, taint, spread impurity in."

If a virus infects your body, it makes copies of itself inside of you. People full of hate may plant bad feelings in others. Infect can refer to ideas or germs. It usually indicates something bad.

[Fictional.] Underline the Latin root," fict" which is part of "fac, fact, fect, fic."

I see two suffixes. The suffix "-ion" is part of the Naughty Ending "-tion" [pg. viii]. It makes the word a thing. The suffix "-al" is also a Naughty Ending. It means "relating to or characterized by something."

This word should mean "relating to or characterized by a thing that is made." Which is the best answer?

Write **fictional** next to "something that is made up, imaginary."

Fictional characters or stories are pretend. They were made up by an author.

[Pulse.] Underline the Latin root," puls" which is part of "pel, puls, to push."

The E at the end of this word is just there for spelling. Words tend to end "-ss" or "-se" so that we do not think the word means "more than one."

This word should mean "to push." Which is the best choice?

Write **pulse** next to "throb, beat, to push blood through blood vessels."

You may have heard of this word before. A doctor or nurse will check your pulse. They are measuring how rapidly the blood is being pushed through your body.

[Facilitate.] Underline the Latin root, "fac" which is part of "fac, fact, fect, fic, to make or do."

I see "-ilitate" at the end of this word. This is a combination of suffixes.

The suffix "-ile" means "relating to, suited for, or capable of."

The suffix "-ity" means "a state or condition."

The suffix "-ate" means "to cause or make."

If we start with "fac" and add "-ile", facile should mean "capable of making or doing." (In Spanish, the word *facil* means "easy.") Dropping the "E" to add "-ity", facility should mean "state or condition that is capable of making or doing," and then dropping the "Y" to add "-ate", facilitate should mean "cause or make a state or condition that is capable of making or doing." Which answer is the best fit?

Write **facilitate** next to "to make easier, less difficult; cause to be doable."

Facilitate means "help, assist" or "to make something easier."

[Impulsive.] Underline the Latin root," puls" which is part of "pel, puls, to push."

I see the prefix "im-" which is a variant of "in-". "Im-" is used before roots starting with B, M, or P, and it means "in, on, or toward." It can also mean "not."

I see the suffix "-ive," which means "causing or making." It changes a word into an adjective. It describes something.

This word should describe something that causes or makes something to be pushed inside. Which is the best choice?

Write **impulsive** next to "pushed from within, swayed by emotions, rash."

If you are impulsive, you do not think through your actions. You react quickly based on your emotions.

[Compel.] Underline the Latin root, "pel" which is part of "pel, puls, to push." ☆

    I see the prefix "com-" which is a variant of "con-". "Con-" means "together, with, jointly." "Com-" is used before "B, M, or P."

    This word should mean "to push together." Do you see a good choice? Should we use a dictionary?

        Write **compel** next to "to drive together (cattle), force (people)."

    This word started as a term for herding cattle. Cattle are pushed together into an area. It is now used mainly to mean "force" and usually refers to people. Someone might compel you to do something that you do not want to do.

[Benefactor.] Underline the Latin root, "fact" which is part of "fac, fact, fect, fic, to make or do." ☆

    I see "bene-" at the beginning. "Bene-" is a prefix meaning "well or good." Think of beneficial or benediction.

    I see the suffix "-or" at the end. The suffix "-or" tends to be used with Latin roots. It means the same thing as the suffix "-er". Both mean "one who."

    This word should mean "one who makes or does good." Which is the best choice?

        Write **benefactor** next to "a well to-do person who makes things easier, supporter, patron."

    A benefactor helps people or does good things, usually by giving money.

[Repulsion.] Underline the Latin root, "puls" which is part of "pel, puls, to push." ☆

    I see the prefix "re-" meaning "back or again."

    I see the suffix "-ion" which is part of the Naughty Ending "-sion." The suffix "-ion" means "act of, state of, or result of." It turns the word into a thing.

    This word should mean "something that pushes back or pushes again." Which answer is best?

        Write **repulsion** next to "the state of being pushed away, driven back, disgusted."

    "My repulsion when I smelled the vomit was overwhelming." I had to back away. The disgusting sight pushed me away.

[Sufficient.] Underline the Latin root, "fic" which is part of "fac, fact, fect, fic, to make or do." ☆

    I see the prefix "suf-" which is a variant of "sub-". It means "under, beneath, or secondary." "Suf-" is used before roots that start with "F."

    I see "-ient" at the end. The I could actually be included with the Latin root. "Fici" is the present tense of the root. The suffix "-ent" is the suffix. It changes the word into a noun or adjective.

    This word should mean "a thing or describe a thing" that "makes or does under." Which is the best answer?

        Write **sufficient** next to "having made up the needed amount; adequate, enough."

Think of having to make enough orange juice to fill a pitcher. If the level of orange juice is under the needed amount, then you keep making it until it rises to the required amount. The amount of orange juice that you have is now "sufficient." Sufficient means "enough."

Movements Review

Look at the pictures. Say the root that goes with the picture, do the movement, and say the meaning.

Write the root and the meaning next to the corresponding picture.

Lesson 4 Multiple Choice

These words all have Latin Roots.

We have sixteen Latin roots listed at the top. Underline the root that you see in the word. Use the movement to help you remember what the root means, and find that meaning in one of the choices below the word.

Expulsion. Underline the Latin root. "Puls" which is part of "pel, puls, to push." Read each choice. Do any of the choices have to do with pushing? If you are still stuck, you could look for other clues. Do you know of any words that start with "ex-"? That might help you make an educated guess about which answer is the best choice. Explode, exterior.

Expulsion. C) the state of being driven out or rejected.

If you break certain rules at school, you might face expulsion. You would get kicked out of the school and have to find another school that is willing to teach you. Think about the guy in our story about the root mit, miss. He faced expulsion from the theater when he was caught throwing popcorn.

Dictum. Underline the Latin root. "Dict" which is part of "dic, dict, to say." Read each choice. Do any of them have to do with speaking?

Dictum. A) something said with authority, a pronouncement.

A dictum is usually a well known saying that is believed to be true. It may be an opinion with authority, but nobody is required to follow it. You may have heard the dictum, "You are what you eat."

Revert. Underline the Latin root. "Vert" which is part of "vert, vers, to turn." Do any of the choices have to do with turning?

Revert. A) return back to a former habit.

If a child is scared, he may revert back to his old habit of sucking his thumb.

Traduce. Underline the Latin root. "Duce" which is part of "duc, duce, duct, to lead." Do any of the choices have to do with leading?

Traduce. C) lead across as a spectacle, scorn, speak badly of.

This term now means "to speak badly of," but it began with the idea of leading someone across a public area so that others could observe bad traits or embarrassing things about him. The word now refers to speaking, but it helps to understand its original usage because it may help you to remember the meaning and the spelling.

Credulous. Underline the Latin root. "Cred, to believe." Do any of the choices have to do with believing?

Credulous. B) willing to believe or trust too readily, gullible.

"He was credulous and believed his toy wand actually made the flowers grow."

Impel. Underline the Latin root. "Pel" which is part of "pel, puls, to push." Do any of the choices have to do with pushing?

Impel C) to drive forward, press on

"The joy of crossing the finish line would impel me to finish the race even though my legs felt numb."

Faction. Underline the Latin root. "Fact" which is part of "fac, fact, fect, fic, to make or do." Do any of the choices have to do with making or doing?

Faction B) a making or doing, a group, a political party, class

This word really just means" a group." It began in Ancient Rome as a group of contractors who made chariot parts. Its association with make or do is less obvious now. It usually refers to a smaller group who disagrees with the majority.

Portage. Underline the Latin root. "Port, to carry." Do any of the choices have to do with carrying?

Portage A) carrying boats and goods over land to water.

When Lewis and Clark could no longer navigate their boats up the river because they came to a waterfall, they had to portage. They had to carry all of their things and their boats over the land until they came to safe water.

Inference. Underline the Latin root. "Fer, to bear or yield." Do any of the choices have to do with bearing or yielding?

Inference. C) a conclusion that has been yielded based on reason.

You make inferences when you read books. If you read that it took three hours to travel from Miami to Atlanta, then you would guess based on facts that you know and experience that you have had, that they used an airplane. You would have to infer this if the mode of travel is not written in the book. An inference involves putting all of the bits of information that you have together to produce or yield a conclusion. It is an educated guess.

Scribacious. Underline the Latin root. "Scrib" which is part of "scrib, spript, to write." Do any of the choices have to do with writing?

Scribacious. A) having a tendency to write too much.

"He had a hard time finding a satisfying ending to his story and so he became a bit scribacious, writing on, and on, and on."

Pretest/Post-test Answers

After completing all four worksheets, please take the post-test and compare your results to the pretest when you finish.

1. trans**form**   A) change shape
2. ex**port**   B) carry away
3. cor**rupt**   A) broken morals
4. **dis**tract   C) draw attention away
5. tran**scribe**   C) make a written copy
6. **spec**tacle   B) a public sight
7. **struct**ure   A) a building
8. in**flect**ion   B) curve in voice pitch

9. **dict**ate   A) tell one what to do
10. coni**fer**   B) bearing pinecones
11. e**mit**   C) send forth
12. aque**duct**   C) device to lead water
13. **cred**ible   B) worthy of belief
14. di**vert**   A) turn from a path
15. pro**puls**ion   B) pushing forward
16. **fac**ile   A) easily done

124

The following is based on the prefix appendix in Unlocking Literacy by Marcia K. Henry. Please consult her book for lists of words using each prefix and learning activities. If a prefix is not included in this list, we recommend you consult www.dictionary.com which breaks words into morphemes and lists origin and history.

Prefixes

Prefixes modify a root.
They do not stand alone.
They are used at the beginning of a word.

Three Kinds of Prefixes

- Some prefixes are only spelled one way and only mean one thing. Students may be able to think of familiar words containing these prefixes to determine what they mean. We will call these Simple prefixes.

- Some prefixes mean more than one thing. Students need to consider both meanings. We will call these Dual or Multi prefixes.

- Some prefixes change the way that they are spelled based on the first letter of the word they are modifying. These different spellings are called variants. We will call these Variant prefixes.

    - Variants explain why there are two Rs in "corrupt."
        - Phonetically, the second R is not required.
        - The first R is part of the prefix "cor-" which is a variant of "con-". This variant is used because "rupt" starts with R. We will call "rupt" an R root.
        - The second R is part of the root "rupt."
    - Noting the morphemes may help students to remember the spelling, and reviewing the variants may help students to recognize the meaning of a common prefix spelled in a different way.
    - Variants can often, but not always, be identified by the doubled consonant.
    - Variants are depicted in boxes on the right of the page. These boxes help students to visualize the complexity or simplicity of a prefix.

The variant is determined by the first letter of the root that the prefix is modifying.

Most of the time this box will indicate the first letter of the root, but sometimes the specific root will be listed.

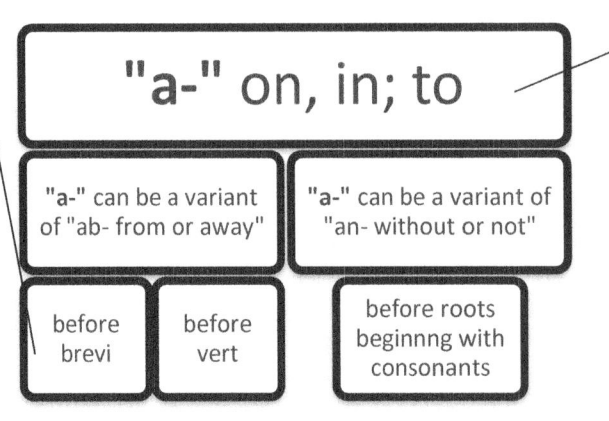

The top box will list the **Base Prefix.** This is the most common meaning of the prefix.

More than one box in the top row indicates multiple meanings.

126

a- on or in; to (Variant/Multi)
   "A-" usually means "on, in; to."
   Variants of other prefixes are also spelled "a-".
   Students must determine if it is:
       (Simple) "a-" on, in; to
       (Variant) of "ab-" from or away
       (Variant) of "an-" without or not.

ab- from or away (Variant)

ad- to, toward, in, near (Variant)

ambi- both (Simple)

an- without or not (Variant)
   "An-" can be a variant of "ad-" to, toward, in or near before N roots.

   The N will be doubled if the variant of "ad-" meaning "toward" is used.

   It will not be doubled if it means "without or not."

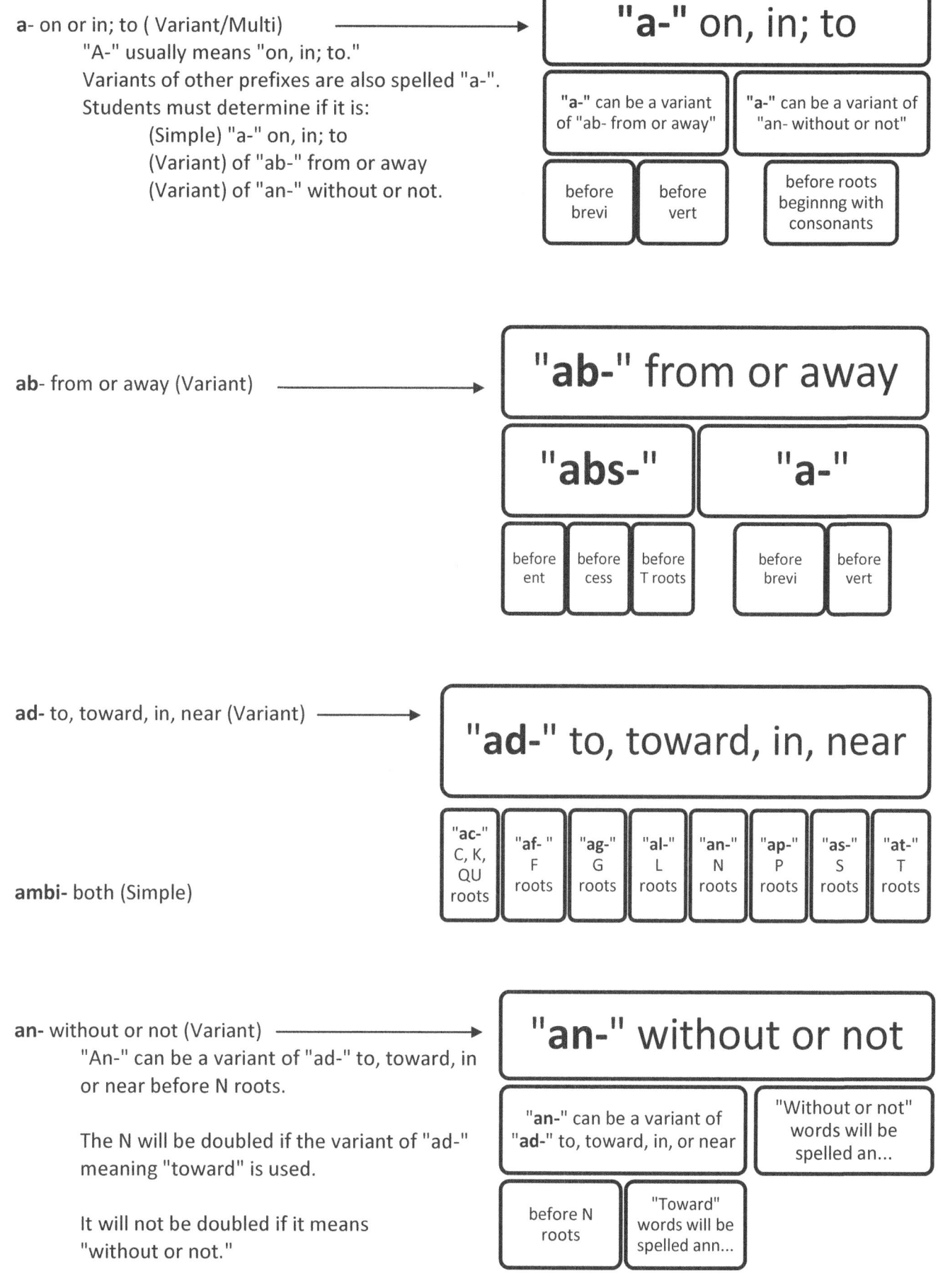

127

ante- before (Simple)

anti- opposite or against (Simple)

be- completely, thoroughly, excessively (Simple)

bene- well or good (Simple)

circum- around or about (Simple)

con- together, with, jointly (Variant)

contra- against, opposite, contrasting (Simple)

counter- contrary, opposite (Simple)

de- down or away from (Simple)

dis- not, absence (Variant)

dys- bad or difficult (Simple)

ex- out or thoroughly (Variant)

fore- before (Simple)

in- in, on, toward; or not (Dual Variant)

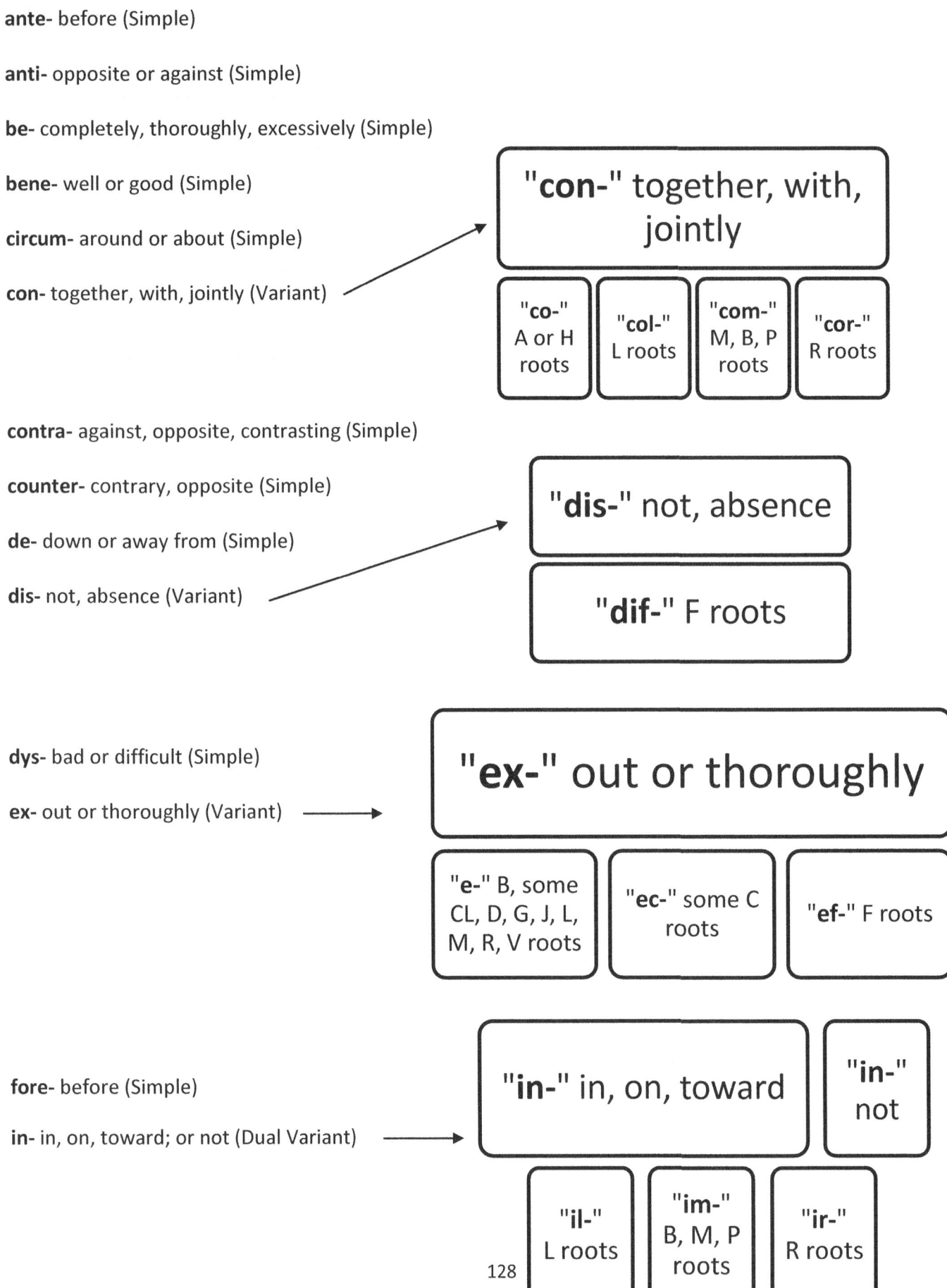

inter- between (Simple)

intra- within (Simple)

intro- in or inward (Simple)

mal- bad, badly; abnormal (Simple)

mid- middle (Simple)

mis- bad, badly, wrong, wrongly (Simple)

multi- many or much (Simple)

non- not or negative (Simple)

ob- (Multi Variant)
- means "extra" (intensifies the root)
- means "down, against facing"
- means "to"

all 3 variants can use all 3 meanings

"**ob-**" extra	"**ob-**" down, against facing	"**ob-**" to
"**oc-**" C roots	"**of-**" F roots	"**op-**" P roots

per- completely or extra (intensifies the root) (Dual)

post- after, behind, following (Simple)

pre- before (Simple)

pro- forward (Simple)

re- back again; or extra (intensifies the root) (Dual)

se- apart, aside, without (Simple)

sub- under, secondary (Variant)

"**sub-**" under, secondary

| "**suc-**" C roots | "**suf-**" F roots | "**sug-**" G roots | "**sup-**" some P roots | "**sus-**" some P or T roots |

syn- together, with (Variant)

trans- across, beyond (Simple)

un- (Multi)
- to undo or reverse
- not
- opposite of

"**syn-**" together, with

| "**syl-**" L roots | "**sym-**" B, M, or P roots |

Number Prefixes

Numerical Order			
1	uni-	100	cent-
	mono-	1,000	mili-
2	bi-		kilo-
	duo-	10,000	myria-
	di-	Million	mega-
3	tri-	Billion	giga-
	ter-	Trillion	tera-
4	quad-, quar-	Quadrillion	peta-
	tetra-		
5	quint-		
	pent-		
6	sex-		
	hex-		
7	sept-		
	hept-		
8	octa-, octo-		
9	nona-, nove-		
10	dec-, deca-, deci-		

Alphabetical Order			
bi-	2	octa-	8
cent-	100	octo-	8
dec-	10	pent-	5
deca-	10	peta-	quadrillion
deci-	10	quadr-	4
di-	2	quar-	4
duo-	2	quint-	5
exa-	quintillion	sept-	7
giga-	billion	sex-	6
hept-	7	ter-	3
hex-	6	tera-	4
kilo-	1,000	tetra-	4
mega-	million/large	tri-	3
mille-	1,000	uni-	1
mono-	1		
myria-	10,000		
nona-	9		
nove-	9		

The following collection of suffixes is based on the appendix found in <u>Unlocking Literacy</u> by Marcia K. Henry. Please consult her book for lists of words containing each suffix as well as suggested learning activities.

Suffixes

Suffixes modify a word's meaning, often by changing its part of speech.

- The roots are usually derived from verbs.
- Suffixes change roots into nouns, adjectives, adverbs, and sometimes back to verbs.
- Words can contain multiple suffixes.
- Bad Breath E is frequently dropped when adding a suffix.
- Words ending in Y.
    - Words in English do not end with "i". The letter "i" is so skinny, it might fall over at the end of a word, so you have to put a brace on it. This brace turns it into a letter "y." In fact, the only word in English that end with "i" is the word "I," and it has a brace on the top and the bottom that keep it from falling over. Think of the words "my", "boy", "day", and "by."
    - Adding a suffix to words ending in Y
        - If Y has a vowel buddy (oy, ay), then the Y remains, as in "toyed, "swayed".
        - If the suffix being added starts with I, then the Y usually remains to avoid "ii," as in "allying," "crying," "lobbyist."
        - Otherwise, remove the brace, changing Y to I before adding a suffix, as in "allied," "cried," lobbied."
- Naughty Endings are made up of the last letter of a root plus a suffix. See page viii in the front of the book for further details regarding Naughty Endings.

-**able:** able, can do; **adj**

-**ade:** result of action; **noun**

-**age:** collection, mass, relationship; **noun**

-**al, -ial:** relating to, characterized by; **adj**

-**an:** relating to; **adj** or **noun**

-**ant:** person of action or state; **noun** or **adj**

-**ar: adj**
    (sometimes these letters just the end a noun
    and are not a suffix: sugar, molar, cigar)

-**ard:** one habitually or excessively in a specified condition; **noun**

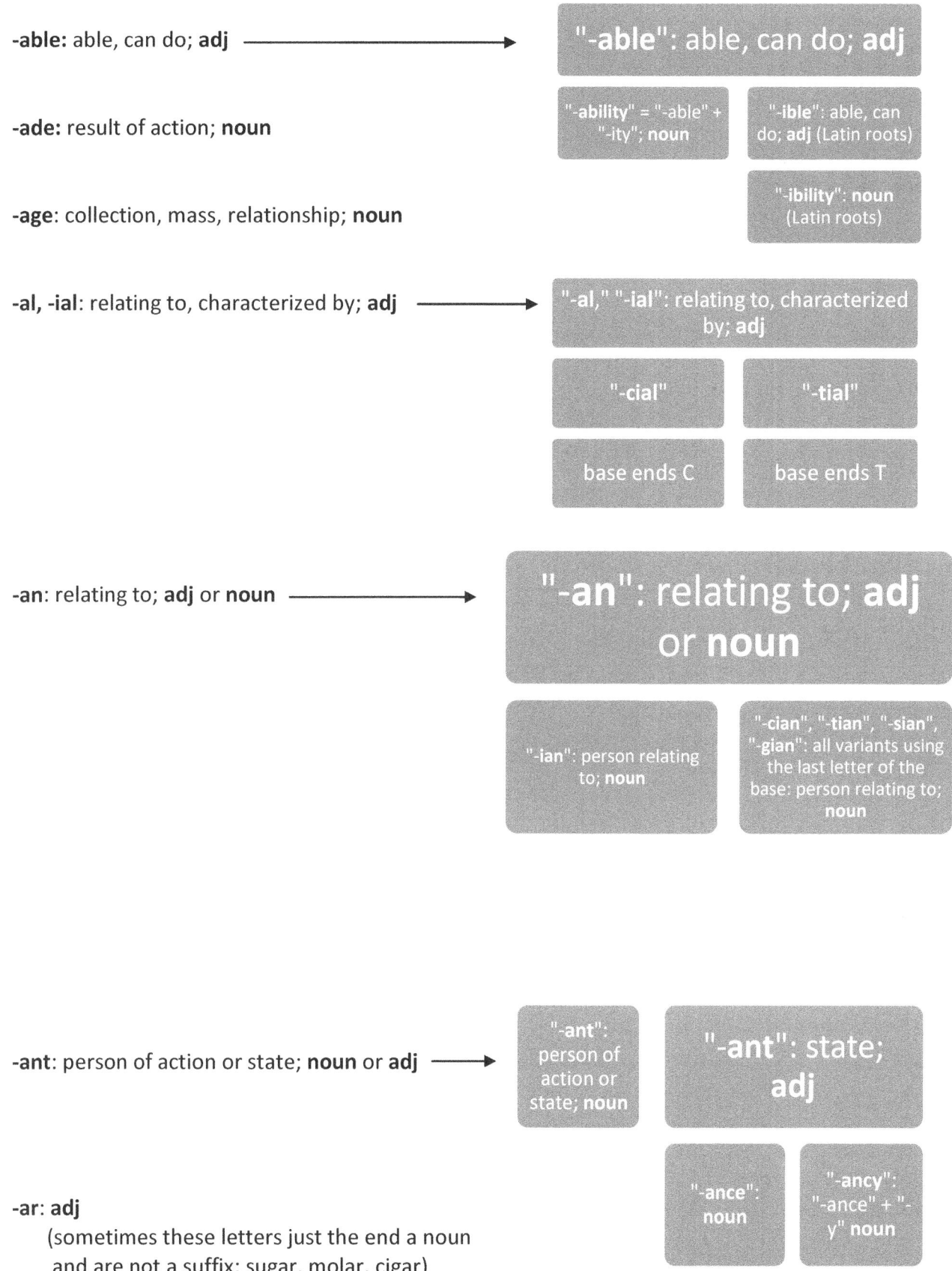

-ary: "-ar" + "-y"
  relating to, place where; **noun**
  adj

-ate:
  cause or make; **verb**
  adj

-cide: kill; **noun**
  (same origin as Latin root cise: to cut)

-cy: state, condition, quality; **noun**

-dom: quality, realm, office, state; **noun**

-ed: past tense; **verb**

-ee: one who receives an action; **noun**

-eer: one associated with; **noun**
  "-ee" + "-er"

-en: made of; **adj**

-ence: action, state of, quality; **noun**

-ency: action, state, quality; **noun**
  "-ence" + "-y"

-ent: referent; **noun**
  adj

-er:
  one who, that which; **noun** non-Latin roots
    same meaning as "-or" Latin roots
  comparative degree, more; **adj**

-ery: relating to, quality, place where; **noun**
  "-er" + "-y"

-ess: feminine; **noun**

-est: superlative degree, most; **adj**

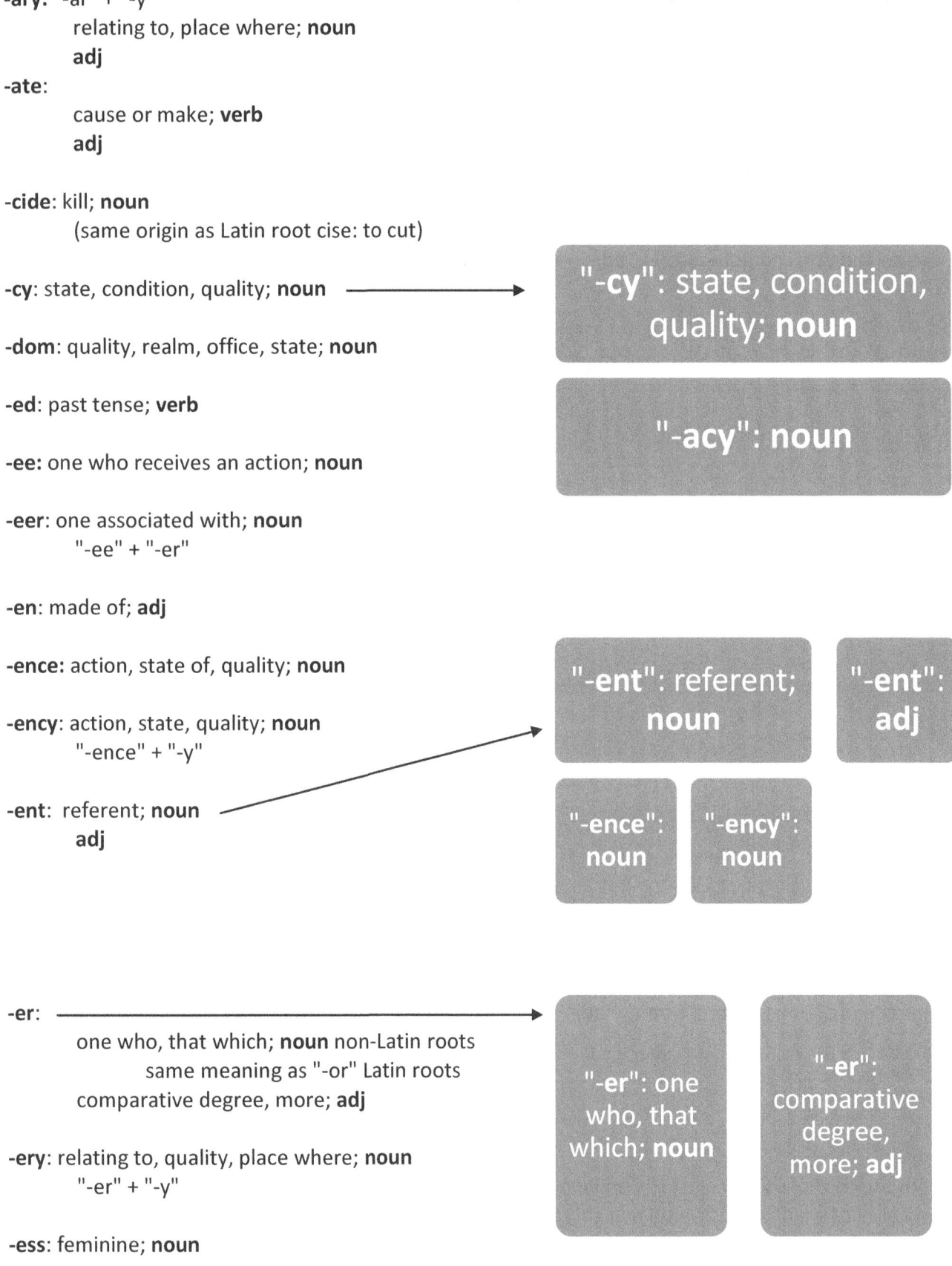

-**ette**: small or diminutive; **noun**

-**fold**: related to a specified amount; **noun**

-**ful**: full of, full; **adj**, **noun**

-**fy, -ify**: make; **verb**

-**hood**: condition, state, quality; **noun**

-**ial, -al**: relating to, characterized by; **adj**

-**ian**: one having a certain skill/art; **noun**

-**ic**: of, pertaining to, characterized by; **adj**

-**ify, -fy**: make; **verb**

-**ile**: relating to, suited for, capable of; **noun**

-**ine**: nature of; **noun, adj**

-**ing**: present tense; **verb**

-**ion**: act of, state of, result of; **noun**

-**ish**: origin, nature, resembling; **adj**

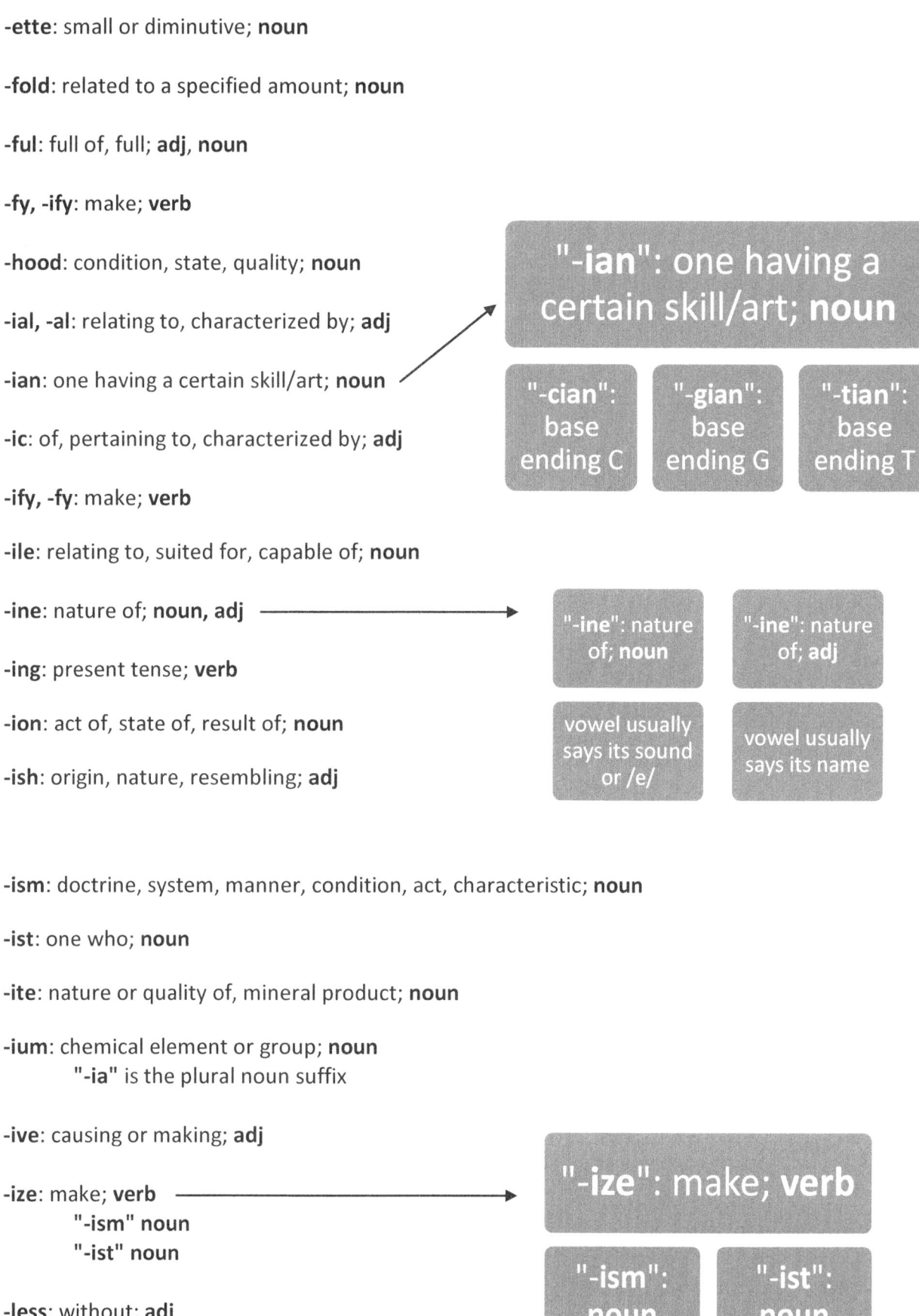

-**ism**: doctrine, system, manner, condition, act, characteristic; **noun**

-**ist**: one who; **noun**

-**ite**: nature or quality of, mineral product; **noun**

-**ium**: chemical element or group; **noun**
    "**-ia**" is the plural noun suffix

-**ive**: causing or making; **adj**

-**ize**: make; **verb**
    "**-ism**" noun
    "**-ist**" noun

-**less**: without; **adj**

-ling: very small; diminutive; **noun**

-logy: science or study of; **noun** ⟶ **"-logy"**: science or study of; **noun**

"-ology"

"-ologist" = -ology + -ist: one who deals with/studies a topic; **noun**

-ly: like or manner; **adj**

-ment: act, state, result of an action; **noun**

-most: most or nearest to; **superlative adj**

-ness: state of; **noun**

-or: who, that which; **noun** (Latin roots)

-ory: "-or" + "-y"
　　relating to, quality place where; **noun**
　　pertaining to, characterized by; **adj**

-ous: full of, having; **adj** ⟶ **-ous**: full of having; **adj**
　　many Naughty Endings formed
　　with the base

-ious, -cious, -gious, -sious, -tious, -xious are all variants using the last letter of the base

-s: **plural noun**
　　"-es" following S, X, CH, SH, Z

-ship: office, state, dignity, skill, quality, profession; **noun**

-some: characterized by a specified quality, condition, or action; **adj**

-ster: one who is associated with, participates in, makes or does; **noun**

-tude: condition, state, quality of; **noun**

-ty, ity: state of or quality of; **noun**

-ure: state of, process, function, office; **noun**
　　"-ture," "-sure"

-ward: expressing direction; **adj**

-y: inclined to; **adj**

References

Brown, J. I. 1947. Reading and vocabulary: 14 master words. In M. J. Herzberg (Ed.), Word study, 1-4. Springfield, MA: G & C Merriam.

The importance of Latin in the English Language is best summarized by this idea: 12 Latin roots plus 2   Greek combining forms could produce 100,000 English words.

www.Dictionary.com

This free website lists definitions, origin, morphemes, and word history.

Heath, Chip and Dan. 2007. Made to Stick: *Why Some Ideas Survive and Others Die*. New York, NY: Random House Publishing.

The SUCCES concept of using stories to make things stick discussed in this book.

Henry, M. K. 2010. Unlocking Literacy: *Effective Decoding and Spelling Instruction, 2nd Edition*. Baltimore, Maryland: Paul H. Brookes Publishing Co.

This book was the missing link to organizing reading and spelling. The selection of roots and their order as well as the prefix and suffix appendixes are based on this outstanding book. Consult this book for further activities and lists of words sharing common prefixes, suffixes, Latin roots, and Greek combining forms.

Lindamood, Patricia C. and Phyllis D. 1998. Lindamood Phoneme Sequencing Program for Reading, Spelling, and Speech *The LiPS Program, 3rd Edition*. Austin, Texas: Pro Ed Inc.

This outstanding phonics system continues to change lives. It is the key to students learning to decode.

www.StevensonLearning.com

This language system contributed to an understanding of phonics rules, particularly hard and soft C and G.

www.WilsonLanguage.com

This language system also contributed to an understanding of phonics rules.

Made in the USA
Middletown, DE
01 July 2025